Terrestrial Vegetation and Soils Monitoring at Casa Grande Ruins National Monument

2008 Status Report

Natural Resource Technical Report NPS/SODN/NRTR—2011/487

Authors

Cheryl L. McIntyre
Sonoran Institute
44 E. Broadway Blvd., Ste. 350
Tucson, AZ 85701

J. Andrew Hubbard
Sarah E. Studd
National Park Service
Sonoran Desert Network
7660 E. Broadway Blvd., Ste. 303
Tucson, AZ 85710

Editing and Design

Alice Wondrak Biel
Sonoran Desert Network
National Park Service
7660 E. Broadway Blvd., #303
Tucson, AZ 85710

September 2011

U.S. Department of the Interior
National Park Service
Natural Resource Stewardship and Science
Fort Collins, Colorado

The National Park Service Natural Resource Stewardship and Science office in Fort Collins, Colorado, publishes a range of reports that address natural resource topics of interest and applicability to a broad audience in the National Park Service and others in natural resource management, including scientists, conservation and environmental constituencies, and the public.

The Natural Resource Technical Report Series is used to disseminate results of scientific studies in the physical, biological, and social sciences for both the advancement of science and the achievement of the National Park Service mission. The series provides contributors with a forum for displaying comprehensive data that are often deleted from journals because of page limitations.

All manuscripts in the series receive the appropriate level of peer review to ensure that the information is scientifically credible, technically accurate, appropriately written for the intended audience, and designed and published in a professional manner. This report received informal peer review by subject-matter experts who were not directly involved in the collection, analysis, or reporting of the data.

Views, statements, findings, conclusions, recommendations, and data in this report do not necessarily reflect views and policies of the National Park Service, U.S. Department of the Interior. Mention of trade names or commercial products does not constitute endorsement or recommendation for use by the U.S. Government.

This report is available from the Sonoran Desert Network website, http://www.nature.nps.gov/im/units/sodn/, as well as at the Natural Resource Publications Management web site, http://www.nature.nps.gov/publications/nrpm/.

Please cite this publication as:

McIntyre, C. L., J. A. Hubbard, and S. E. Studd. 2011. Terrestrial vegetation and soils monitoring at Casa Grande Ruins National Monument: 2008 status report. Natural Resource Technical Report NPS/SODN/NRTR—2011/487. National Park Service, Fort Collins, Colorado.

NPS 303/109705, September 2011

Contents

Figures

Tables

Executive Summary

This report summarizes the Sonoran Desert Network's first season of terrestrial vegetation and soils monitoring at Casa Grande Ruins National Monument (NM), in south-central Arizona. In 2008, six permanent field-monitoring sites were established and sampled across two units: the Casa Grande unit and the proposed Adamsville unit. Our objectives were to determine the status of and detect trends, over five-year intervals, in vegetation cover, vegetation frequency, soil cover, and surface soil stability.

Our results revealed a shrubland dominated by creosote bush (*Larrea tridentata*), as is common in low-elevation valley bottoms of the Sonoran Desert. The Casa Grande Ruins unit site contained a near-monoculture of creosote bush, whereas the Adamsville unit had greater perennial plant diversity, including the presence of triangle burr ragweed (*Ambrosia deltoidea*), littleleaf ratany (*Krameria erecta*), and yellow paloverde (*Parkinsonia microphylla*).

Preventing the spread of exotic plants is an important management goal at the park. While we did not document any invasive plants on our plots, recent surveys have identified 31 exotic invasive plants at Casa Grande Ruins NM, although the rates of occurrence and density were low relative to other Sonoran Desert parks. Therefore, we recommend continued vigilance toward potential invasions of exotic plant species.

The park, as a whole, appears to be free of substantial soil erosion, although a few sites had evidence of rill and gully development. Soil surfaces are currently moderately well-armored, with less than 15% of the soil surface consisting of unprotected, bare mineral soil. However, a substantial portion of the soil surface is covered by early stage cyanobacteria biological soil crusts, which are moderately more resistant to water and wind erosion than bare soil but do not provide as much protection as lichen and moss biological soil crusts, rocks, and plant bases. In addition, surface soil aggregates are relatively stable. However, the stability of surface aggregates collected from bare soil was relatively low, suggesting the potential for soil loss from bare patches. As soil erosion has important consequences for natural and cultural resources at the park, this is an important consideration.

Within the context of the network's vital signs for species composition, community structure, and dynamic soil function, we conclude that terrestrial vegetation and soils at Casa Grande Ruins NM are within the range of natural variability given the groundwater depletion in the area since the early 1900s. While current park conditions stand in contrast to those described in local and regional historic accounts (recognizing the limitations of historical data), the valley-wide groundwater declines that began in the early 1900s due to irrigated agriculture have likely changed the potential vegetation at Casa Grande Ruins NM, making some differences inevitable.

Acronyms

AVG	average
GRTS	Generalized Random Tessellation Stratified
MDC	minimum detectable change
N	number
NM	national monument
NPS	National Park Service
RRQRR	Reversed Randomized Quadrant-Recursive Raster
SD	standard deviation
Sdiff	standard deviation of the differences
SE	standard error
SODN	Sonoran Desert Network

Acknowledgements

We thank Casa Grande Ruins NM staff Rebecca Carr, Sheldon Baker, and Superintendent Jason Lott for their on-site support of the field effort and the overall Sonoran Desert Network (SODN) Inventory and Monitoring Program. Kate Connor, Beth Fallon, Laura Crumbacher, Scot Pipkin, Betsy Vance, and Sheldon Baker conducted the field data collection, often under arduous conditions. Betsy Vance and Scot Pipkin carefully processed all of the soil samples. Expert data processing and management was completed by SODN Data Manager Kristen Beaupré, and Lindsay Fitzgerald-DeHoog updated the master plant lists.

1 Introduction

1.1 Background

Generating more than 99.9% of Earth's biomass (Whittaker 1975), plants are the primary producers of life on our planet. Vegetation therefore represents much of the biological foundation of terrestrial ecosystems, and it comprises or interacts with all primary structural and functional components of these systems. Vegetation dynamics can indicate the integrity of ecological processes, productivity trends, and ecosystem interactions that can otherwise be difficult to monitor. Land management actions often focus on manipulating vegetation to achieve park management objectives, with defined conditions based on community structure or lifeform composition.

In the Sonoran Desert ecoregion (Bailey 1998), vegetation composition, distribution, and production are highly influenced by edaphic factors, such as soil texture, mineralogy depth, and landform type (McAuliffe 1999). Especially as they relate to water, these influences are magnified at local scales, as described by pioneering desert ecologist Forrest Shreve: "The profound influence of soil upon desert vegetation is to be attributed to its strong control of the amount, availability and continuity of water supply. This fundamental requisite in plants is the most effective single factor in the differentiation of desert communities" (Shreve 1951). As such, a fundamental understanding of soils and landforms is essential for evaluating vegetation patterns and processes (McAuliffe 1999).

The Sonoran Desert Network (SODN), as part of the National Park Service's Inventory and Monitoring (I&M) Program, has identified terrestrial vegetation and dynamic soil functional attributes as important ecosystem monitoring parameters, or "vital signs" (NPS 2005) that provide key insights into the integrity of terrestrial ecosystems at Casa Grande Ruins National Monument (NM; Figure 1-1). Indicators of terrestrial vegetation integrity include vegetation community structure, lifeform abundance, status and trends of established exotic plants, and early detection of previously undetected exotic plants. Indicators of soil dynamic function and erosion resistance include the cover of mineral soil and the stability of surface soil aggregates.

1.2 Goals and objectives

The overall goal of the SODN terrestrial vegetation and soils monitoring program is to ascertain broad-scale changes in vegetation and dynamic soils properties in the context of changes in other ecological drivers, stressors, ecological pro-

Figure 1-1. Typical winter-rainy season vegetation, Casa Grande unit, Casa Grande Ruins National Monument. Note dead mesquite (*Prosopis velutina*) in the foreground.

cesses, and focal resources of interest. This integrated approach explores patterns and identifies candidate explanations to support effective management and protection of park natural resources in a cumulative fashion, such that the results of each successive round of monitoring builds upon the knowledge gained from previous efforts and related research and monitoring activities.

Specific, measurable objectives for SODN terrestrial vegetation and soils monitoring (Hubbard et al. in review) at Casa Grande Ruins NM are to determine the status of and detect trends in (over five-year intervals):

1. Terrestrial vegetation cover for common (≥10% absolute canopy cover) perennial species, including non-native plants, and all plant lifeforms.

2. Terrestrial vegetation frequency of uncommon (<10% absolute canopy cover) perennial species, including non-native plants.

3. Terrestrial soil cover by substrate classes (bare soil, litter, vegetation, biological soil crust, rock fragments of several size classes) that influence resistance to erosion.

4. Terrestrial soil stability of surface aggregates by stability class (1–6).

5. Basal cover and frequency of biological soil crusts by morphological group.

1.3 Scope

This document reports and interprets the results of the first round of terrestrial vegetation and soils monitoring at Casa Grande Ruins NM. Our focus is necessarily on current status, with trend evaluations to commence after the next sampling period in 2013. We do, however, contrast these current results with those from previous studies and interpret the information in the context of management objectives and ecological considerations.

1.4 Study area

1.4.1 Park establishment and purpose

Located approximately 70 miles northwest of Tucson and 60 miles southeast of Phoenix, Casa Grande Ruins NM is the fifth-oldest unit in the National Park Service and was the first prehistoric and cultural preserve established in the United States (NPS 2011a). The monument was authorized in 1889, and a June 22, 1892 proclamation by President Benjamin Harrison created Casa Grande Ruin Reservation to protect the Casa Grande, a four-story adobe structure that was built by the Hohokam between AD 1200 and 1450. The General Land Office managed the Casa Grande Ruin Reservation until 1918, though the transfer of management began following the creation of the National Park Service in 1916 (Clemensen 1992). On August 3, 1918, President Woodrow Wilson proclaimed Casa Grande a national monument to ensure the "protection, preservation and care of the ancient buildings and other objects of prehistoric interest thereon" (Wilson 1918). Potential expansion of the monument includes the prospective Adamsville unit and several small parcels of land near the current monument boundary.

Casa Grande Ruins NM contains 61 documented prehistoric archeological sites on its 472.5 acres. The monument also includes 15 historic structures eligible for listing on the National Register of Historic Places. Only three of the Hohokam-period sites are open to the public. The remaining archeological sites, which require a special-use permit or ranger guide, are managed as backcountry sites, providing their natural and cultural resources with a level of protection from human impacts (NPS 2011a). Between 2000 and 2009, the monument averaged 93,600 visitors per year (NPS 2011b).

1.4.2 Biogeographic and physiographic context

Casa Grande Ruins NM is located within the Basin and Range physiographic province, characterized by nearly level valley floors surrounded by mountain ranges (Figure 1-2). Mountain ranges near the monument are isolated and consist of pre-Cambrian granite and schists (Clemensen 1992). The monument is close to four mountain ranges: the San Tan Mountains, four miles to the north; the Sacaton Mountains, 10 miles to the west; the Picacho Mountains, 20 miles to the southeast; and the Casa Grande Mountains, 20 miles to the southwest. The monument drains into the McClellan Wash, a tributary of the intermittent Gila River, which flows 1.5 miles north of the monument.

Casa Grande Ruins NM also lies within the Sonoran Desert Ecoregion, spanning 55 million acres in Arizona, California, Baja California, and Sonora. With elevations ranging from 1,414 to

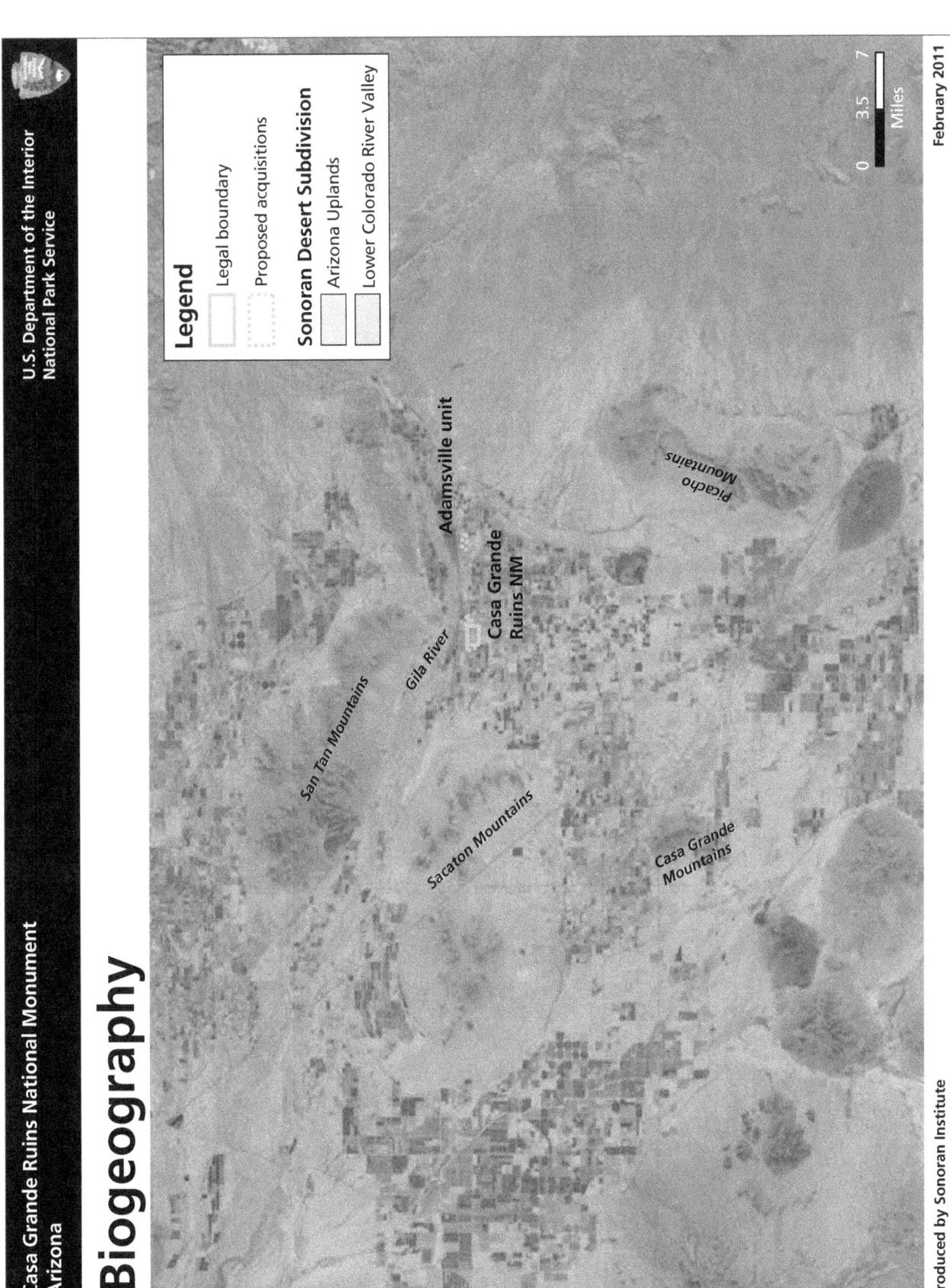

Casa Grande Ruins National Monument
Arizona

U.S. Department of the Interior
National Park Service

Biogeography

Legend

Legal boundary

Proposed acquisitions

Sonoran Desert Subdivision

Arizona Uplands

Lower Colorado River Valley

San Tan Mountains

Gila River

Adamsville unit

Casa Grande Ruins NM

Sacaton Mountains

Picacho Mountains

Casa Grande Mountains

0   3.5   7

Miles

February 2011

Produced by Sonoran Institute

Figure 1-2. Biogeographic map of Casa Grande Ruins NM.

1,427' (Clemensen 1992), the monument falls within the Lower Colorado River Valley Subdivision of the Sonoran Desert and within the desert biome. Valleys within the Lower Colorado River Valley Subdivision are dominated by creosote bush-white bursage. The vegetation community within the desert biome contains a variety of phreatophytic (deep-rooted) shrubs, such as mesquite (*Prosopis* spp.) and creosote bush (*Larrea tridentata*). Succulents are ubiquitous, with agave (*Agave* spp.), yucca (*Yucca* spp.), barrel cactus (*Ferocactus* and *Echinocactus* spp.), hedgehog cactus (*Echinocereus* spp.), and prickly pear and cholla (*Opuntia* spp.) common (Dimmit 2000).

1.4.3 Vegetation

Vegetation characterization and mapping efforts conducted at the monument in 2007–2008 revealed 15 distinct types, with a total of 35 species recorded during sampling efforts (Buckley et al. 2009) (Table 1-1). The creosote bush shrubland alliance dominated the main unit of Casa Grande Ruins NM. Of all the community types described at Casa Grande Ruins NM, two had corresponding alliance types recognized by NatureServe, and one had a corresponding association. None of the other six proposed types had a global alliance-or association-level description or code within the current NatureServe explorer database (Buckley et al. 2009).

1.4.4 Local geology and soils

The monument lies on an alluvial deposit composed of Quaternary age gravel, sand, and silt (Reichhardt 1992). The alluvium thickness increases from 400 feet at the Gila River to more than 1,200 feet in Coolidge; alluvium at the monument is approximately 800–1,200 feet thick. Soils at and near the monument are classified as Hyperthermic Arid soils, which have a mean annual soil temperature of higher than 22°C (72°F) and receive less than 10 inches of annual precipitation on average (Hendricks 1985).

Coolidge sandy loam is the dominant soil type within the current monument boundary, comprising over 80% of the soil, with the remainder being the Laveen loam soil type (Figure 1-3). Both soil types have less than 15% rock fragments by volume, are considered well-drained, and have a slight risk of water erosion. Coolidge soils typically have a calcic horizon at depths between 14 and 40 inches. The soils at the proposed expansion areas adjacent to and near the current monu-

ment are also Laveen loams and Coolidge sandy loams. At the proposed Adamsville unit, there are four soil map units: Coolidge sandy loam; Denure sandy loam (1–3% slopes); Gunsight-Pinamt complex (1–8% slopes); and Laveen loams. The Gunsight-Pinamt complex soils have 35–60% rock fragments by volume. Soil properties have important consequences for vegetation composition, persistence, and productivity (McAuliffe 1999). Therefore, we explored relationships between in situ soil characteristics and vegetation monitoring parameters in a complementary effort (Nauman in review).

1.4.5 Biological soil crusts

Open spaces on the soils at Casa Grande Ruins NM are typically covered by biological soil crusts, a community of cyanobacteria, algae, lichens, and bryophytes.

Biological soil crusts provide key ecosystem functions, such as increasing water and wind erosion resistance, contributing organic matter, and fixing atmospheric nitrogen. In the Sonoran Desert, cyanobacteria dominate the crust community. Cyanobacteria weave through the upper few millimeters of soil, binding together soil particles by secreting polysaccharides. In addition to reducing water erosion, the polysaccharides contribute to soil aggregate structure, which is directly correlated with soil erosion resistance (Belnap et al. 2003; Herrick et al. 2005b). Mosses and lichens have small, anchoring structures that help them protect the soil surface (Belnap et al. 2003). On most soils, biological soil crusts increase infiltration. However, on soils with more than 80% sand-sized particles, biological soil crusts tend to reduce infiltration rates (Warren 2003).

Biological soil crusts contribute fixed carbon to soil through decaying and leaching processes (Lange 2003). Cyanobacteria and cyanolichens have the ability to fix atmospheric nitrogen. This process reduces atmospheric nitrogen (N_2) to ammonia (NH_4^+), which is usable by vascular plants (Belnap 2003). Biological soil crusts can be the dominant source of nitrogen for desert ecosystems. The distribution and species composition of biological soil crusts is influenced by soil chemistry and disturbance (Belnap et al. 2001).

Lichens are a composite, symbiotic organism composed of a fungus and either a cyanobacteria or a green algae. In general, lichens with the same growth form have similar ecological functions.

Table 1-1. Vegetation alliances and associations mapped at Casa Grande Ruins National Monument and the proposed Adamsville expansion, 2007–2008.

Map class	Common name	Area (hectares)		
		Monument	Adamsville	Total area
Woodland				
Prosopis velutina / Larrea tridentata Woodland Alliance (P)	Velvet mesquite / Creosotebush Woodland Alliance	0	1.71	1.71
Prosopis velutina Woodland Alliance	Velvet mesquite Woodland Alliance	0	0.9	0.9
Wooded Shrubland				
Parkinsonia microphylla / Larrea tridentata Wooded Shrubland (P)	Foothills paloverde / Creosotebush Wooded Shrubland	0	16.4	16.35
Shrubland				
Larrea tridentata - [Ambrosia deltoidea-Krameria erecta] Shrubland (P)	Creosotebush - [Triangle burr ragweed - Littleleaf ratany] Shrubland	0	23.6	23.6
Larrea tridentata - Lycium fremontii Shrubland Alliance (P)	Creosotebush - Fremont's wolfberry Shrubland Alliance	5.63	0	5.63
Larrea tridentata Shrubland Alliance	Creosotebush Shrubland Alliance	162.3	19.7	182
Sparse Shrubland				
Larrea tridentata / Mixed Annual Sparse Shrubland (P)	Creosotebush / Mixed Annual Sparse Shrubland	12.77	0	12.77
Sphaeralcea ambigua Sparse Shrubland Alliance (P)	Desert globemallow Sparse Shrubland Alliance	0	8.58	8.58
Anderson Land Use Classes				
Transitional areas	Transitional Areas	33.68	0	33.68
Agriculture	Agriculture	60.77	7.45	68.22
Horticulture	Horticulture	3.46	0	3.46
Non-vegetated	Non-vegetated	1.48	0	1.48
Park Facilities	Park Facilities	3.85	0	3.85
Transportation	Transportation	0	3.85	3.85
Mixed Urban or Built-up Land	Mixed Urban	53.7	4.75	58.45

P = proposed
Table from Buckley et al. (2009)

Squamulose lichens provide the most protection of the soil from water erosion, followed by crustose, foliose, and fruticose lichens. Gelatinous lichens provide the least protection from water erosion. Having some vertical growth allows lichens to provide additional protection from wind erosion by increasing surface roughness and decreasing the erosive power of wind. Crustose and gelatinous lichens are effective at resisting detachment but do not provide as much resistance to wind erosion as other growth forms. All gelatinous lichens fix nitrogen, whereas nitrogen fixation is species-dependent for the other growth forms. Following disturbance, gelatinous lichens tend to recover relatively quickly, followed by crustose, squamulose, foliose, and fruticose lichens. Bryophytes, which also occur on the soil surface, are small, non-vascular plants, including mosses and liverworts.

The recovery of biological soil crusts from disturbance depends on factors such as the climatic regime and type of disturbance. Generally, crusts recover slowly in areas with high annual temperature and low annual precipitation (Belnap and Eldridge 2003), such as Casa Grande Ruins NM. Biological soil crusts follow a recovery sequence in which, typically, cyanobacteria first colonize a site, followed by cyanolichens, other lichens, and then moss (Belnap et al. 2001).

1.4.6 Site and soil stability

Site stability is the resistance of a site to localized wind and water erosion of soils—with tremendous consequences for park ecosystems and the

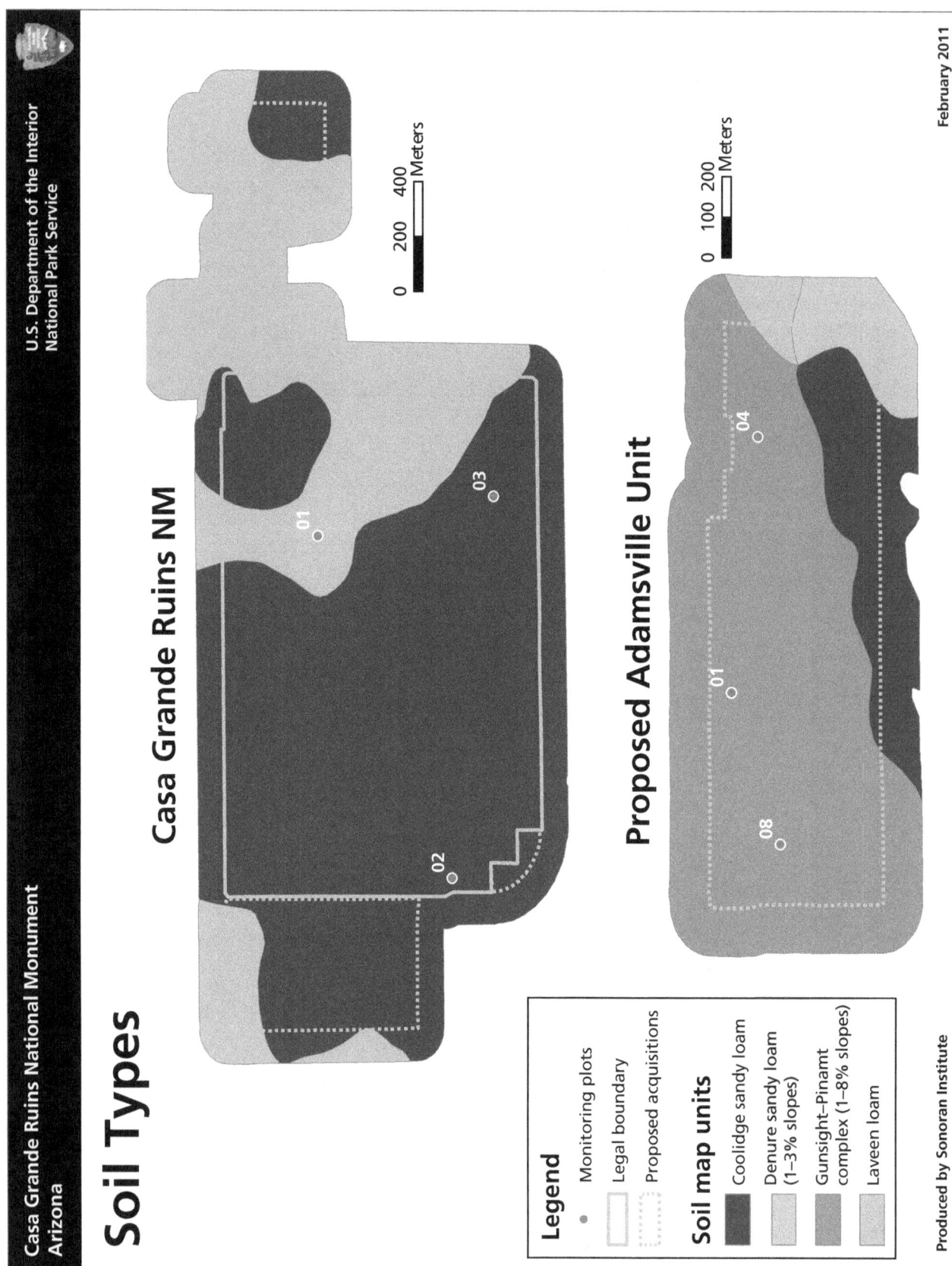

Figure 1-3. Map of the soil types of Casa Grande Ruins NM.

protection of finite aboveground and subsurface cultural resources.

Soil factors mediate water relations for plants in semi-arid environments (McAuliffe 1990), thereby controlling patch-scale ecological composition and net primary productivity (Herrick et al. 2005b). As recovery of disturbed soils is particularly slow in dry and seasonally dry environments (Aber and Melillo 1991), avoiding erosion is of paramount importance to effective natural resource management in SODN parks, including Casa Grande Ruins NM.

Static and dynamic factors determine the vulnerability of a site to water erosion (Herrick et al. 2005b). Static factors are generally not affected by management actions and include soil texture, depth and parent material, slope, aspect, and climate (Herrick et al. 2005b). These factors can be combined to estimate site erosion potential (Davenport et al. 1998). Static factors set the range of erosion potential within which dynamic factors may be influenced by disturbance and management action to determine actual erosion.

Dynamic factors that affect water erosion include soil disturbance, soil structure, total cover, and plant basal cover. The amount of total cover (soil cover and vegetation cover) is the single most important dynamic factor affecting water erosion (Herrick et al. 2005b). Most soil loss occurs in "unprotected" areas with uncovered bare soils (Davenport et al. 1998), whereas rock, gravel, vegetation, biological soil crusts, and even plant debris (litter and duff) can "armor" the soil, slowing the flow of water and permitting increased infiltration of water into the soil profile (Belnap et al. 2007).

1.4.7 Climate

Casa Grande Ruins NM experiences climate typical of the Sonoran Desert Ecoregion: highly variable, bimodal precipitation with a considerable range in daily and seasonal air temperature and relatively high potential evapotranspiration rates (Ingram 2000). Approximately 40% of the annual precipitation falls during summer thunderstorms from July through September (NCDC 2011), when maximum air temperatures can exceed 40°C and lead to violent (and often localized) rainstorms. The thunderstorms are highly variable in time and space and primarily derive their moisture from the Gulf of California and the tropical Pacific Ocean (Sheppard et al. 2002).

The bulk of the remaining annual precipitation falls in relatively gentle events of broad extent from November through March (Ingram 2000). Because the winter storms originate in the Pacific Ocean, sea-surface temperatures affect the amount of winter precipitation. In El Niño years, sea-surface temperatures in the eastern Pacific Ocean near the equator are warmer than normal and the Sonoran Desert receives more precipitation than average. In contrast, La Niña years have lower than average winter precipitation due to cooler sea-surface temperatures. Sea-surface temperatures in the northern Pacific Ocean also influence winter precipitation. The Pacific Decadal Oscillation (PDO) can last for several decades when the temperatures in the northern Pacific Ocean are warmer or cooler than usual. When the PDO has warmer than normal temperatures, the Sonoran Desert experiences increased winter precipitation (Sheppard et al. 2002). Occasionally, tropical storms move into the Sonoran Desert in early fall. While infrequent, tropical storms have produced some of the largest rainfall events recorded and can result in widespread flooding and severe erosion (Ingram 2000).

To determine departure from baseline climate conditions, seasonal and annual precipitation are compared to the average precipitation received during a historic or "normal" period (Gray 2008). The most recent 30-year normal computed for the weather station at Casa Grande Ruins NM spans 1971–2000. Therefore, the monthly precipitation and temperature data from 2003–2008 are presented in the context of that time period (Figure 1-4; NCDC 2011).

1.4.8 Human habitation

Archaic people appeared in the Southwest around BC 5500. As hunters and gatherers, they depended on wild animals and plants. Subsistence agriculture began around BC 1000, with the cultivation of small cob popcorn. Beans, such as pinto, red, and navy, were introduced around BC 350. The attention required to produce sufficient crop yields decreased the mobility of the hunter/gathers and initiated the slow transition to a hydraulic culture (Clemensen 1992).

By AD 300, the Hohokam culture appeared and utilized irrigation to support its agriculture. Hohokam is a Pima Indian term meaning "those who have gone." Archeologists divide the Hohokam culture into four periods: Pioneer (AD 300–750); Colonial (AD 750–950); Sedentary (AD 950–

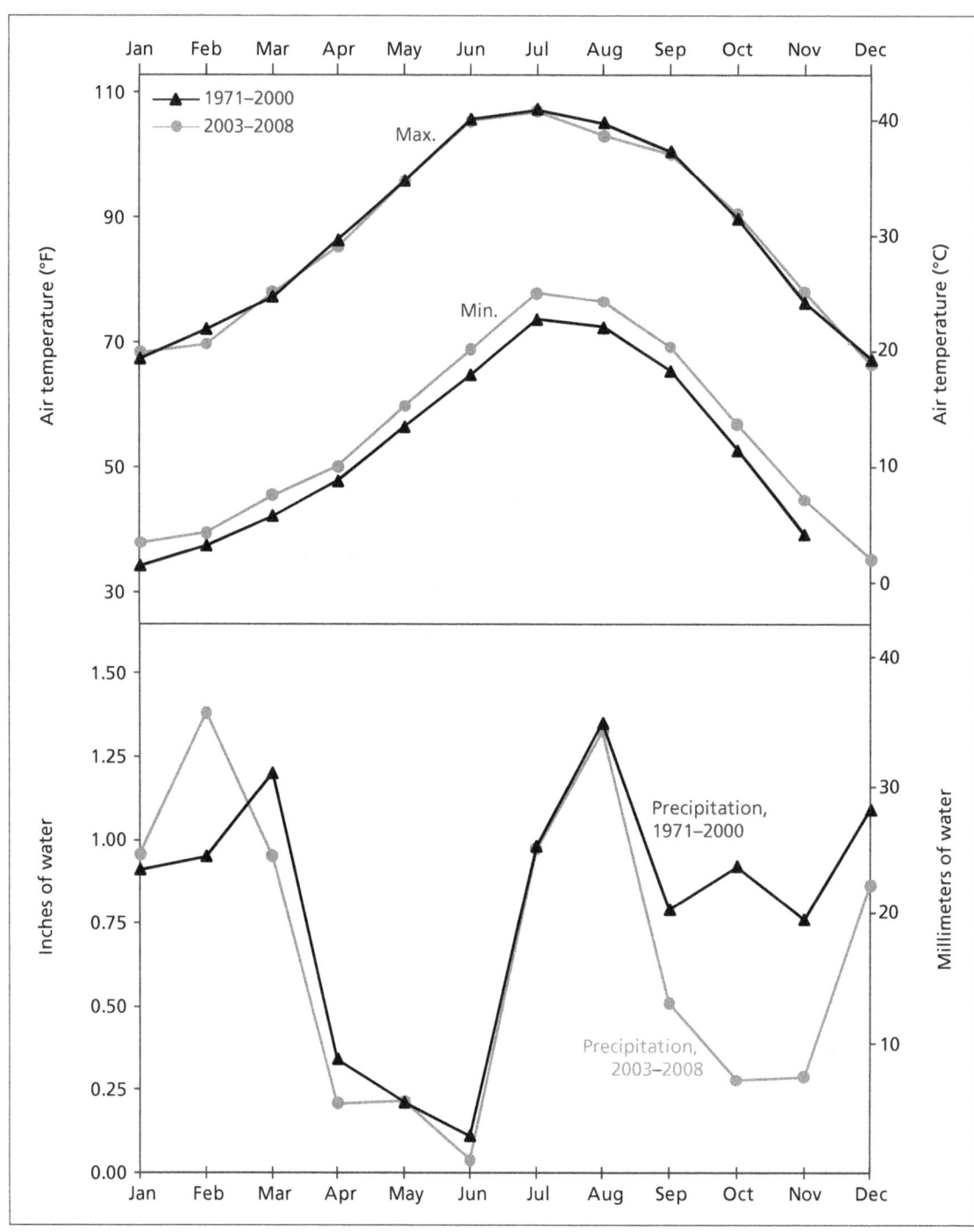

Figure 1-4. Monthly precipitation and temperatures compared to 30-year normal (1971–2000), Casa Grande Ruins NM, 2003–2008 (NCDC 2011).

1175); and Classic (AD 1175–1450). During the Pioneer period, the Hohokam lived in a series of small villages along the middle Gila River (Figure 1-5). As simple farmers, the Hohokam located villages where they found arable land, a shallow aquifer, and a convenient location from which to tap the Gila River for irrigation water. A shallow aquifer was important so that wells need not be more than 10 feet deep. Irrigation canals served only a small village and were of simple construction. From AD 300 to 500, the Hohokam acquired cultivated plants from Mexico, including cotton, teparay beans, sieve and jack beans, and pigweed. During the Pioneer period, the Hohokam supplemented their diet with saguaro fruit and seeds, prickly pear cactus fruit and pads, cholla buds, grass and mustard seeds, and coyote melons, among other desert plants. The Hohokam also hunted small game and fished and clammed in the Gila River (Clemensen 1992).

Population increased during the Colonial period, with resulting increases in some village sizes and refinement of the social system. The larger settlements had ball courts. Population continued to increase during the Sedentary period, which brought numerous changes to the Hohokam civilization. The Hohokam developed a more complex canal system that served more than one village. The canal system altered society because it necessitated leadership to coordinate water distribution, resulting in elite classes. During the Classic period, the population stabilized and shifted toward fewer but larger villages that contained a central or civic-ceremonial district. At Casa Grande Ruins NM, the ball court and community plaza were within the central district, surrounded by Compounds A, B, C, and D. The consolidation of canals by AD 1300 resulted in the centralization of managerial/religious authority in a few villages, which likely could be identified by "Great Houses," such as the Great House at Casa Grande Ruins NM (Clemensen 1992).

During AD 1200–1350, periodic high flows in the Gila River caused the channel to deepen. The periods of high flow were interspersed with periods of low flow, resulting in insufficient amounts of water being diverted into the Hohokam canal intakes. The Hohokam had to move their canal intakes further upstream, increasing the challenge of farming and resulting in the consolidation of some canals. The Casa Grande canal was eventually consolidated and extended to reach a point on the Gila River 18 miles northeast of the village.

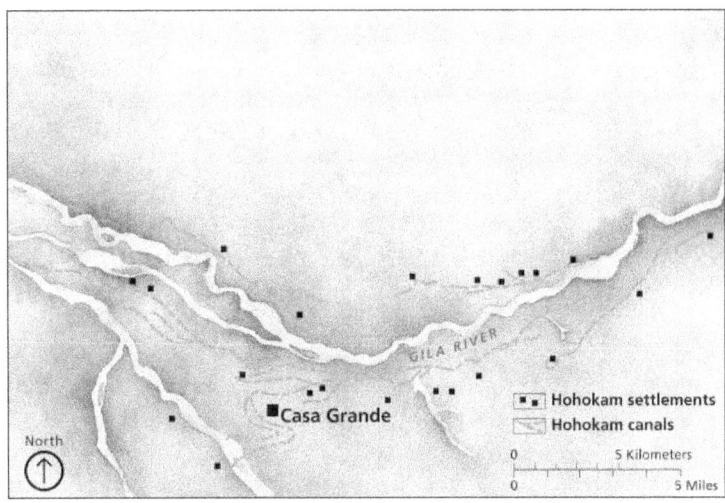

Figure 1-5. Hohokam settlements and canals in the area of Casa Grande Ruins NM.

Disastrous flooding occurred after AD 1350, and the Hohokam abandoned their large settlements between AD 1355 and 1450, as groups moved into the desert or established small villages along the Gila River (Clemensen 1992).

During the roughly 400 years of sparse human habitation following the Hohokam abandonment of Casa Grande, desert vegetation recovered. Euro-American settlement increased following the Gadsden Purchase in 1853. The desert plants, particularly the tall mesquite, impressed travelers in the mid-to-late 1800s. One account from 1879 described mesquite hiding the Great House from view until one was nearly upon it (distance unspecified). An 1869 survey noted the presence of mesquite, greasewood, and grass; the latter had attracted ranchers to the area by the early 1870s, and cattle ranching prospered for roughly 50 years. The livestock impacted local natural and cultural resources. Early custodians of Casa Grande Ruins reported that cattle, likely attracted by the shade provided by the structures, rubbed against the ruins and trampled over the mounds. The cattle also grazed vegetation around the ruins and trampled plants and soils. In 1902, custodian Frank Pinkley reported that cattle had consumed all forage within 100 yards of the Great House. The monument was grazed until 1934, when a fence enclosed the monument and prevented large animals from entering (Clemensen 1992). Today, the monument is surrounded by agricultural, commercial, and residential development.

1.4.9 Irrigated agriculture

Irrigated agriculture returned to the Casa Grande area in the 1880s, when farmers began to settle and build diversion dams along the Gila River. Farmers also tapped into groundwater in the Gila Valley. The construction of the Coolidge Dam in the 1920s, its above-ground storage of Gila River water, and an influx of settlers led to agricultural expansion in the area surrounding Casa Grande Ruins NM. The increase in irrigation efforts prompted Frank Pinkley to write, in 1924, that "the time may come when we (Casa Grande Ruins NM) will have the only bit of typical desert land in this part of the valley" (Clemensen 1992). In 1932, C. P. Russell observed that agriculture surrounded the monument on all sides, making it a sort of native desert preserve.

Growth and irrigation continued to increase from 1930 to 1945. As settlers found the water stored behind the Coolidge Dam to be insufficient for their needs, they drilled wells to supplement the water supply. This groundwater pumping rapidly lowered the water table, causing farmers to drill deeper wells. In 1942, the depth to groundwater at the monument was 88 feet; by 1945, it had increased to 102 feet. The water table continued to drop, falling to 140 feet in 1948. Speculation of impending water-use regulations in the late 1940s prompted land speculators to drill as many wells as possible in advance of new regulations. During 1950, the water table varied between 163 and more than 186 feet (the bottom of the Casa Grande Ruins NM well), prompting the monument to connect to the Arizona Water Company in 1952. The water table in the Casa Grande area reportedly dropped to 300 feet in 1956. The increasing depth to groundwater levels, combined with drought, led to the abandonment of some agricultural fields beginning as early as 1947 (Clemensen 1992). In 1992, approximately 21% of the land within 30 kilometers of Casa Grande Ruins NM was classified as agricultural. Slightly less land (20%) was classified as agricultural in 2001 (NPS 2010a).

1.4.10 Urban development

Casa Grande Ruins NM lies within a mosaic of agricultural, commercial, and residential development. The monument is located within the city of Coolidge, which saw an increase in population from 7,786 inhabitants in 2000 to an estimated 11,079 inhabitants in 2009 (USCB 2011). The Pima Lateral Canal borders the south side of the monument and the Southern Pacific Railroad runs to the east. The monument is bordered by roads—Highway 87 to the north and Highways 87/287 to the east. Highway 287 runs through the proposed Adamsville unit (Figure 1-6). Several large-scale commercial developments, along with smaller stores and restaurants, are located just east of the monument, along Highways 87/287. The south and southwest portion of the monument adjoin residential developments. Currently, agriculture abuts the north and west sides of the monument.

1.4.11 Brief overview of natural resource inventories

As part of the I&M Program, 12 basic natural resource inventories were authorized and funded through the National Park Service for all 270 parks deemed to have significant natural resources (NPS 2009). At time of writing, eight of these inventories had been completed for Casa Grande Ruins NM, two were nearly complete, one was being updated, and the last was expected to be completed at a future date (Table 1-2). Coordinated at the national level, most of these inventories rely on existing information and deliver products ranging from electronic data sets to short reports. However, three inventories involved extensive fieldwork culminating in detailed reports: species lists, lists of species occurrence and distribution, and vegetation characterization.

1.4.12 Other long-term monitoring and related ecological research

In addition to terrestrial vegetation and soils monitoring, the Sonoran Desert Network conducts long-term monitoring on birds, climate, exotic plants, and groundwater at Casa Grande Ruins NM. Details on these efforts are provided by the National Park Service (NPS; NPS 2005) and on the Sonoran Desert Network website, http://science.nature.nps.gov/im/units/sodn/.

Casa Grande Ruins NM has also been the focus of other ecological research relevant to terrestrial vegetation and soils monitoring. From 1939 to 1942, regional naturalist Natt Dodge and park ranger Francis Elmore collected 43 plant species from throughout the monument. These specimens are stored at the University of Arizona Herbarium (Powell et al. 2006). Reichhardt (1992) surveyed plants at the monument in 1987, classified vegetation communities, and generated a map of vegetation communities following Brown

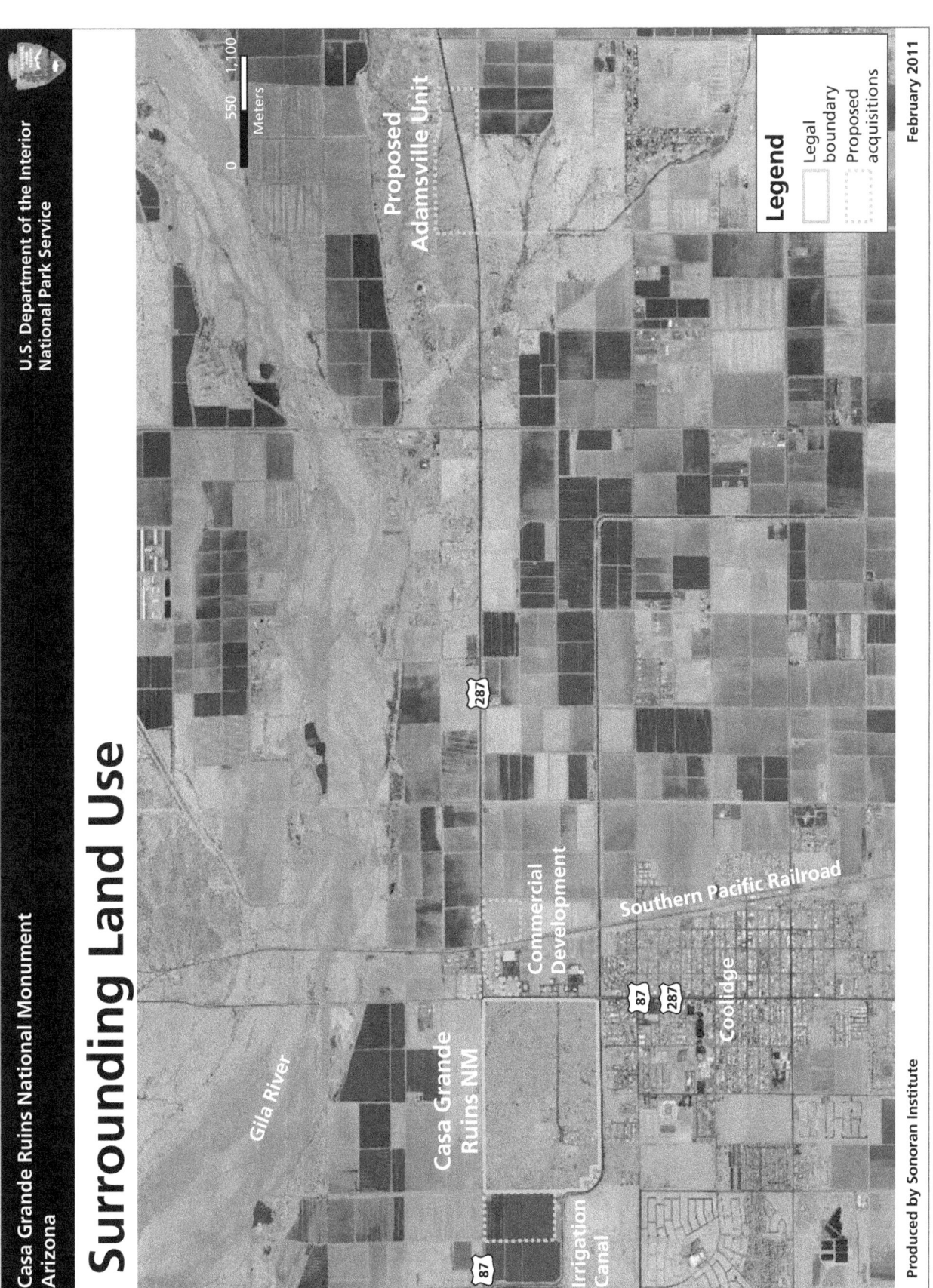

Casa Grande Ruins National Monument
Arizona

U.S. Department of the Interior
National Park Service

Surrounding Land Use

Gila River

Casa Grande Ruins NM

Commercial Development

Southern Pacific Railroad

Coolidge

Irrigation Canal

Proposed Adamsville Unit

287

87

287

87

0 550 1,100

Meters

Legend

Legal boundary

Proposed acquisitions

Produced by Sonoran Institute

February 2011

Figure 1-6. Satellite imagery of Casa Grande NM shows a patchwork of agricultural fields and commercial and residential development as well as an irrigation canal, railroad, and highways.

Table 1-2. Status (2011) of natural resource inventories for Casa Grande Ruins National Monument.

Inventory	Description	Status (2011)
Air Quality Data	Baseline air quality data collected both on and off-park. *Products:* http://www.nature.nps.gov/air/maps/AirAtlas/	Complete
Air Quality Related Values	An evaluation of resources sensitive to air quality. *Products:* http://www.nature.nps.gov/air/Permits/ARIS/	Update
Base Cartographic Data	A compilation of basic electronic cartographic materials. *Products:* http://science.nature.nps.gov/nrdata/	Complete
Baseline Water Quality	Assessment of water chemistry in Middle and West Forks of Gila River. *Products:* http://www.nature.nps.gov/water/horizon.cfm	Complete
Climate	A basic assessment of nearby climate stations and instrumentation. *Products: http://www1.nrintra.nps.gov/NPClime/*	Complete
Geologic Resources	A synthesis of existing geologic data, resulting in a report and electronic map. *Products:* http://www.nature.nps.gov/geology/inventory/	Map complete, report in progress
Natural Resource Bibliography	An electronic catalog of natural resource-related information. *Products:* http://science.nature.nps.gov/im/apps/nrbib/	Complete
Soil Resources	Electronic geospatial data regarding basic soil properties. *Products:* http://www.nature.nps.gov/geology/soils/	In progress
Species Lists Species Occurrence and Distribution	Documentation of the occurrence and distributions of >90% of the vertebrates & vascular plant species, based on prior research and fieldwork. *Products:* Powell and others (2007)	Complete
Vegetation Characterization	Description, classification, and mapping of vegetation communities, based on fieldwork. *Products:* http://science.nature.nps.gov/im/units/sodn/	Complete
Water Body Location and Classification	Basic geographic data on hydrologic units.	In progress

and others (1979). Reichhardt (1992) also compiled a checklist of non-ornamental plants, established vegetation monitoring plots and photo points, and mapped the locations of live mesquite trees (*Prosopis* sp.). Powell and others (2006) provided a more comprehensive review of natural resource research at Casa Grande Ruins NM.

1.5 Issues of concern

1.5.1 Surrounding land use

As described in Section 1.4.7, the monument lies within a mosaic of agricultural, residential, and commercial development. The agricultural fields are potential vectors for non-native invasive plants, such as red brome (*Bromus rubens*) and Johnsongrass (*Sorghum halepense*). In addition, periodic dredging of the Pima Lateral Canal results in sediment deposition, likely containing non-native plant seeds, along the monument boundary (NPS 2005).

To maintain high yields, farmers typically use pesticides and herbicides. Because the insects killed by these chemicals are the primary food source for many animals, the loss or contamination of insects may cause mortality, impaired health, or abandonment of the area by animals, such as birds (Powell et al. 2006). Drift, or overspray, from the aerial application of herbicides and pesticides (which began in the 1950s) (Clemensen 1992) can adversely affect the monument's vegetation (Powell et al. 2006).

Residential and commercial developments and their associated roads may impact the monument by (1) increasing non-native plants, such as ornamental fountaingrass (*Pennisetum setaceum*); (2) increasing trash; (3) increasing runoff by increasing the amount of impermeable surfaces and decreasing the water quality of runoff due to toxins from vehicles; (4) disrupting animal movement patterns through mortality and modification of animal behavior; and (5) increasing mortality and harassment of native animals due to free-roaming pets (Powell et al. 2006). Residential development and housing density are expected to continue to increase in the area surrounding Casa Grande Ruins NM (Figure 1-7). According to housing density projections provided by the NPScape landscape dynamics program, approximately 60% of the private land subject to development within 30 kilometers of Casa Grande Ruins NM was developed by 2000, mostly at a low density of less than

1.5 housing units per square kilometer. By 2020, both the amount of land developed and the housing density are expected to increase, with more than 80% of the available land being developed. Over time, housing density in the area is expected to increase, with most of the developed land having between 50 and 145 housing units per square kilometer by 2060. The amount of land impacted by commercial and industrial development is expected to remain stable between 2000 and 2100. These housing-density projections assume that land not vulnerable to development in 2000, such as federal and state lands, will remain free of development over time (NPS 2010b).

1.5.2 Groundwater depletion

A century of groundwater use for agricultural, residential, and commercial uses lowered the groundwater table around Casa Grande Ruins NM. Cones of depression formed in areas of groundwater pumping, which altered the flow of groundwater (NPS 2005). In some areas, earth fissures and land subsidence have formed due to the compaction of alluvium following groundwater removal (Reichhardt 1992). While fissures and land subsidence have not occurred at Casa Grande Ruins NM, there are examples nearby. The nearest known fissure is approximately 10 miles from the monument, at Black Butte; the nearest documented land subsidence is five miles south of the monument, at Randolph. By 1978, the land surface had dropped one meter (Reichhardt 1992). While water tables rose in recent years, the potential for subsidence at the monument, which could threaten the Great House, remains a concern (NPS 2005).

The rapid decline of groundwater levels in the early twentieth century likely affected the monument's vegetation. Mesquite in the area declined rapidly beginning in 1931. A 1936 infestation of mistletoe and insect attacks concerned monument personnel and prompted two studies of the monument's mesquites. Nearly all of the mesquites at Casa Grande Ruins NM had died by the 1960s. A 1971 study concluded that the lowered water table and mistletoe infestation were the primary drivers of the decline, with insect infestation, age, and lack of reproduction as secondary factors (Clemensen 1992). Climatic conditions, such as drought, may also have played a role in the mesquite decline. Today, mesquite are sparse within the monument and tend to occur naturally in areas where surface runoff collects (Buckley et al. 2009).

Housing Density Near Casa Grande Ruins NM

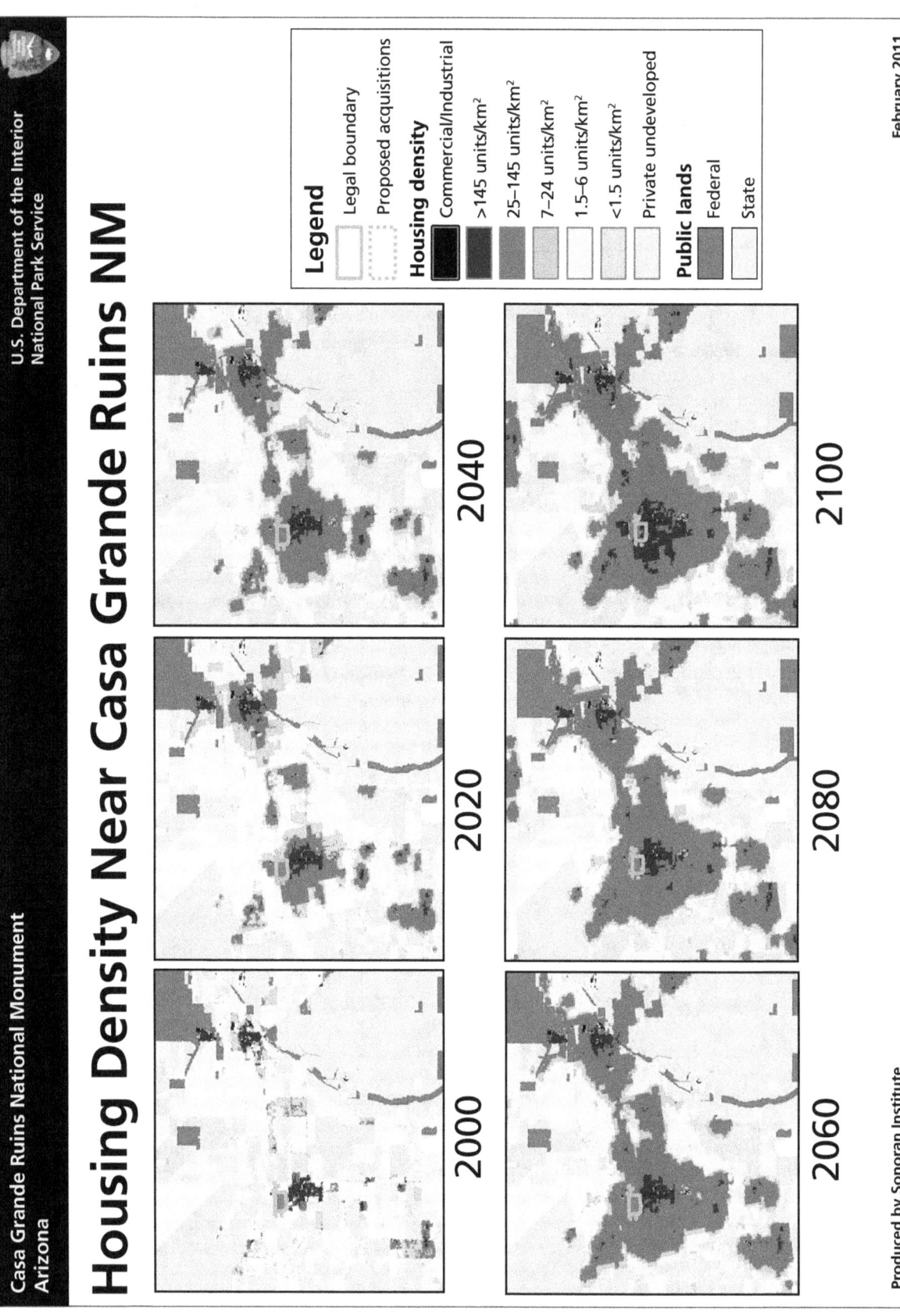

Legend

Legal boundary
Proposed acquisitions

Housing density
Commercial/Industrial
>145 units/km²
25–145 units/km²
7–24 units/km²
1.5–6 units/km²
<1.5 units/km²
Private undeveloped

Public lands
Federal
State

2000

2020

2040

2060

2080

2100

Produced by Sonoran Institute

February 2011

Figure 1-7. Housing density projections from 2000 to 2100 in the area surrounding Casa Grande Ruins NM. Projections courtesy of the Spatially Explicit Regional Growth Model (SERGoM) through the NPScape landscape dynamics program. Projections assume that land not eligible for development in 2000, such as federal and state lands, will remain free of development over time.

1.5.3 Invasive exotic plants

Biological invasions into new regions, whether accidental or deliberate, have increased at unprecedented rates in the past few hundred years (D'Antonio and Vitousek 1992). Once established, non-native plant species often lead to changes in ecosystem processes that are self-maintaining and evolving, leading to functional as well as compositional change. Several studies have implicated environmental and climatic variables as potential drivers for sustaining or accelerating non-native plant dominance in semi-arid ecosystems (Shinneman and Baker 2009). In the American Southwest, historic and current land-use practices, such as livestock grazing and fire suppression, are thought to have contributed to the susceptibility of arid lands to invasion and subsequent loss of native species, as well as decreased biodiversity (Brown and Archer 1999).

As part of the USGS Weeds in the West project (Halvorson and Guertin 2003), the presence and abundance of 50 pre-selected introduced plants were assessed and mapped in Arizona. During that survey effort (1999–2001), 29 non-native, introduced plant species were recorded at Casa Grande Ruins NM, 12 of which were grasses (Table 1-3). Most of the other species were forbs, with one tree/shrub: tree tobacco (*Nicotiana glauca*). In 2002–2003, the NPS (Powell et al. 2006) recorded 12 invasive exotic plants during a vascular plant inventory, all of which were also found by Halvorson and Guertin (2003) (Table 1-3).

During 2006, the NPS, Sonoran Institute, and citizen scientists from the Arizona-Sonora Desert Museum mapped the spatial location, abundance, and distribution of the plants on the Arizona Wildlands Invasive Plant Working Group species list (Studd and McIntyre 2007) (Table 1-3). During that effort, 17 non-native species were recorded, including two species that were not directly observed by Halvorson and Guertin (2003) or Powell and others (2006): barnyard grass (*Echinochloa crus-galli*) and saltcedar (*Tamarix* spp.).* Many non-native species were introduced to the park as a direct result of human activities, such as past settlement, grazing, farming, excavation, and construction activities.

Exotic plant encroachment typically occurs in two phases: (1) colonization, the process by which a problematic species gradually disperses into suitable habitats, recruits into the system and competes for resources with other members of the plant community; and (2) domination, the process by which, via asymmetrical competition (often mediated through disturbance), the new species becomes common or even dominant in the plant community, often with negative consequences for ecosystem structure and function. It is important to note that the second phase often requires a specific set of ecological triggers or conditions that may in fact never occur (this is why many exotic species are relatively innocuous under some environmental conditions). Determining which phase has occurred is crucial to developing successful management strategies and effective monitoring designs.

1.5.4 Natural/cultural resource conflicts

Native and non-native species have damaged and threatened cultural resources at Casa Grande Ruins NM since the early 1930s. Even mammals and birds that might not normally be considered pests threaten archeological sites by burrowing, nesting, feeding, and roosting on or near the sites (NPS 2011a). Species that particularly threaten cultural resources and human health and safety at Casa Grande Ruins NM include, but are not limited to, round-tailed ground squirrels (*Spermophilus tereticaudus*), house finches (*Carpodacus mexicanus*), common pigeons (*Columba livia*), and European starlings (*Sturnus vulgaris*).

The acidic urine and fecal matter of birds damages the monument's archeological sites by reacting with their alkaline walls. This is especially a concern where fecal matter and urine concentrate, such as at nesting and roosting sites. Park managers are also concerned about the potential impacts of nesting material in the viga sockets of the Great House. Burrowing mammals dig up and displace archeological resources, in some cases exposing them to water, wind, and theft, and disrupt the artifact layering, which provides important archeological context. Rodent burrows can also undermine the bases of prehistoric structures. In some cases, rodents have been observed burrowing beneath modern encapsulation materials to get to the relatively softer prehistoric walls. The burrows can be up to 18 inches below the surface and 10 feet long, which undermines soil surface stability and can result in cave-ins when people walk across the unseen burrows (NPS 2011a).

---

*Reichardt (1992) observed tamarisk growing along the northeast portion of the road adjacent to the canal.

Table 1-3. Non-native invasive plants detected at Casa Grande Ruins NM, 2003–2007.

Species	Common name	2003[a]	2006[b]	2007[c]
Avena fatua	wild oats	present		not present
Boerhavia coccinea	scarlet spiderling	present		non-target species
Brassica tournefortii	Sahara mustard	present	present	present
Bromus carinatus	California brome	present		non-target species
Bromus rubens	red brome	present	present	present
Centaurea melitensis	Malta starthistle	present		present
Chenopodium murale	nettleleaf goosefoot	present	present	non-target species
Conyza sp.	horseweed	present		non-target species
Cynodon dactylon	Bermuda grass	present		present
Descurania sophia	flixweed	present		non-target species
Dimorphotheca sinuata	African daisy	present		non-target species
Echinochloa crus-galli	barnyard grass	not present		present
Eragrostis lehmanniana	Lehmann lovegrass	present		not present
Erodium cicutarium	redstem filaree	present	present	present
Hordeum leporinum	wild barley	present	present	non-target species
Hordeum vulgare	common barley	present		present
Lactuca serriola	prickly lettuce	present		non-target species
Malva parviflora	little mallow	present	present	non-target species
Melilotus spp.	sweetclovers	present	present	present
Nicotiana glauca	tree tobacco	present	present	present
Pennisetum ciliare	buffelgrass	present		not present
Phalaris minor	little seed	present	present	present
Polygonum aviculare	prostrate knotweed	present		non-target species
Salsola sp.	Russian thistle	present		present
Schismus arabicus	Arabian schismus	present	present	present
Schismus barbatus	Mediterranean grass	present		present
Sisymbrium irio	London rocket	present	present	present
Sonchus asper	spiny sowthistle	present	present	present
Sorghum halepense	Johnsongrass	present		present
Tamarix sp.	saltcedar	not present		present
Tribulus terrestris	puncturevine	present		not present

a Halvorson and Guertin (2003)
b Powell et al. (2006)
c Studd and McIntyre (2007)

The number of birds roosting and nesting in the Great House appeared to increase dramatically during the 1990s, when five gallons of bird debris fell onto the ruin floors every week. Burrowing round-tailed ground squirrels began to become problematic in the mid-twentieth century (Swann et al. 1994) and are the subject of debate (Hubbard et al. 2007).

Efforts to control round-tailed ground squirrels, a native species, illuminate a conflict between management objectives: preserving the ruins versus protecting the native species and ecosystem processes. Much of the controversy has centered on the control methods employed, and the efficacy of those methods, rather than on the overall management objectives (Hubbard et al. 2007). To address these issues, Casa Grande Ruins NM recently developed an Environmental Assessment of its Integrated Pest Management Plan (NPS 2011a).

2 Methods

2.1 Response design

The response design for this protocol employs permanent, 20 × 50-m sampling plots (Figure 2-1, Appendix A). The 50-m edges of the plot run parallel with the contours of the site. Vegetation sampling is done in conjunction with soil cover and stability measures along six transects within the plot. In the spaces between transects (subplots), within-plot frequency is estimated by noting the occurrence of any plant species or lifeform not observed on the adjacent transects. See Hubbard and others (in review) for details on plot configuration and data collection.

2.1.1 Vegetation and soil cover: Line-point intercept

Line-point intercept is a common and efficient technique for measuring the vegetation cover of plants. Line-point intercept measures the number of "hits" of a given species out of the total number of points measured (Elzinga et al. 1998; Bonham 1989). Vegetation was recorded within three height categories along each of the six transects using the line-point intercept method, with points spaced every 0.5 m (240 points total). The three height categories were field (0.025–0.5 m), subcanopy (>0.5–2.0 m), and canopy (>2.0 m). Perennial vegetation was recorded to species. Annual vegetation was recorded to lifeform, with the exception of a suite of annual non-native plants that were recorded to the species level. Soil cover was recorded by substrate class (e.g., rock, gravel, litter; see SOP #4, Hubbard et al. in review). Biological soil crust cover was recorded to morphological group (light cyanobacteria, dark cyanobacteria, lichen, moss; see SOP #7, Hubbard et al. in review).

2.1.2 Vegetation frequency: Subplots

The area between any two adjacent transects formed the boundary of 10 × 20-m subplots that were used to estimate within-plot frequency of perennial plant species, exotic plants, and all lifeforms. The occurrence of any species/lifeform that was not measured on the adjacent line-point transect was recorded to determine a within-plot frequency of 0–5. Figure 2-1 shows the relationship between each subplot and its corresponding adjacent transect.

2.1.3 Soil aggregate stability

Surface soil aggregate stability was measured using a modified wet aggregate stability method (Herrick et al. 2005a). Within each plot, samples were collected at 48 pre-determined points on either side of the six line-point intercept transects. The dominant vegetation canopy cover and substrate cover at each point were determined. If the dominant substrate cover was dark cyanobacteria crust, lichen-dominated biological soil crust, or moss-dominated biological soil crust, then the soil surface was not disturbed and the sample was automatically scored in the highest stability category. For all other substrates, a uniformly sized (2–3 mm thick and 6–8 mm on each side) sample was collected and samples were tested in groups of 16. Each sample was placed on a screen and soaked in water for five minutes. After five minutes, the samples were slowly dipped up and down in the water, with the remaining amount of soil recorded as an index of the wet aggregate stability of the sample. Samples were scored from 1 to 6, with 6 being the most stable.

2.1.4 Biological soil crust cover and frequency: Point-quadrats

In addition to line-point intercept measurements, biological soil crust cover was measured using 0.25-m² quadrats. Three quadrats were measured per transect using the point-quadrat method (similar in concept to line-point intercept), with 16 intercept measurements per quadrat, resulting in 18 quadrats and 288 measurements per plot. At each intercept, biological soil crusts were recorded as light cyanobacteria, dark cyanobacteria, bryophytes (moss and liverworts), and lichens by species. The observer then visually surveyed the quadrat for any species or morphological group that was present. Soil-crust frequency by lichen species and morphological group was determined by the number of quadrats occupied relative to the total number of quadrats (i.e., 18). The SODN terrestrial vegetation and soils monitoring protocol (Hubbard et al. in review) provides a detailed description of the point-quadrat methodology. The initial round of sampling at Casa Grande Ruins NM will help SODN to determine differences between the line-point intercept and point-quadrat methodologies.

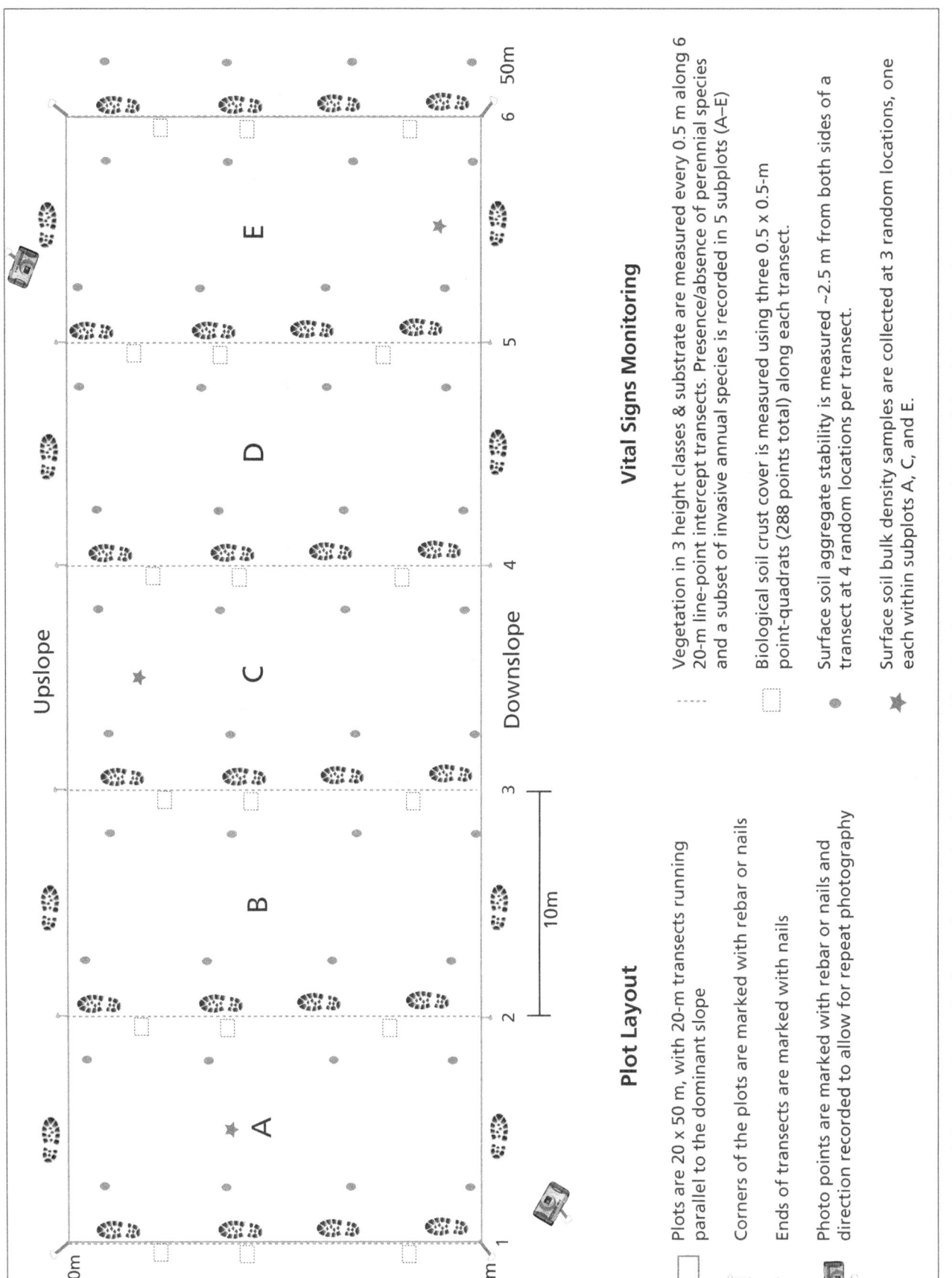

Plot Layout

☐ Plots are 20 × 50 m, with 20-m transects running parallel to the dominant slope

╱ Corners of the plots are marked with rebar or nails

╵ Ends of transects are marked with nails

👢 Photo points are marked with rebar or nails and direction recorded to allow for repeat photography

Vital Signs Monitoring

┄ Vegetation in 3 height classes & substrate are measured every 0.5 m along 6 20-m line-point intercept transects. Presence/absence of perennial species and a subset of invasive annual species is recorded in 5 subplots (A–E)

☐ Biological soil crust cover is measured using three 0.5 × 0.5-m point-quadrats (288 points total) along each transect.

● Surface soil aggregate stability is measured ~2.5 m from both sides of a transect at 4 random locations per transect.

★ Surface soil bulk density samples are collected at 3 random locations, one each within subplots A, C, and E.

Figure 2-1. Terrestrial vegetation and soils monitoring plot design. See Hubbard and others (in review) for additional details on design and data collection.

2.1.5 Soil and site characterization

Proximate soil and landform factors are known to influence vegetation and dynamic soil function parameters at local scales (McAuliffe 1999). To characterize the soil and landscape attributes of each plot, a suite of topoedaphic variables were collected through site diagrams, repeat photo points, and collection of soil cores. Landform, slope position, and parent material were recorded at each plot. Flow-length diagrams were used to depict surface flow patterns and document the slopes (%) and lengths (m) of the hillslope within and immediately upslope of each plot. Permanent photo points were established at each plot corner to characterize general site physiognomy and as an aid to interpreting quantitative trend data in successive sampling periods. In addition, general site descriptions (including observed disturbances such as fire) were collected for each plot.

2.2 Sampling design

2.2.1 Overview

All plots are sampled in late January through March of the same year, and then revisited at five-year intervals. If a major disturbance (e.g., an extended drought, extreme frost, significant soil erosion event, major fire) occurs in the intervening years, we may collect additional plot data to characterize and account for the potential effects of these important stochastic events.

Three permanent monitoring plots (Figure 2-2) were allocated within each of two areas: the current boundary of Casa Grande Ruins NM (Casa Grande unit) and the proposed Adamsville unit (Adamsville unit). Plots for the former were allocated in a spatially balanced arrangement (see Section 2.2.2); the smaller size (~50 ha) of the latter precluded the need for spatial balance. Sample sizes are based on a priori expectations of required sample size to meet our criteria for statistical power and detectability (see Sections 2.2.5–2.2.6).

Terrestrial vegetation and soils plots were allocated using a combination of elevation intervals and soil rock-fragment classes (see Section 3.2.3, Hubbard et al. in review). All areas within the Casa Grande unit occur within one strata (101, <2,500' in elevation), with all surface soils containing <35% rock fragments. Because the Adamsville Unit is ~50 ha, stratification was not

used. Therefore, inference from the plots at Casa Grande Ruins NM is to all terrestrial areas of the park by unit (Casa Grande and Adamsville), except for the areas discussed in Section 2.2.3.

2.2.2 Spatial balance

The spatial sampling design for this protocol employs permanent, 20 × 50-m sampling plots, allocated through a Reversed Randomized Quadrant-Recursive Raster (RRQRR) spatially balanced design (Theobald et al. 2007), using the "spatially balanced sample" function in the STARMAP Spatial Sampling Toolbox in ArcGIS 9.0 (http://www.spatialecology.com/htools/index.php). This tool produces a design that is spatially well-balanced, probability-based, flexible, and simple (Theobald et al. 2007). Because it tries to maximize the spatial independence between plots, the spatially-balanced sampling design should provide more information per plot, thus increasing efficiency (Theobald et al. 2007).

Spatially balanced designs, such as RRQRR (for polygon data) and the Generalized Random Tessellation Stratified (GRTS; for points and lines) approach (Stevens and Olsen 2004), are increasingly being applied to ecosystem monitoring (e.g., Environmental Protection Agency Ecological Monitoring and Assessment Program) because they provide the advantages of a probabilistic design (Stehman 1999) they also ensure spatial balance regardless of overall sample size. RRQRR designs facilitate adding or removing sites in a spatially balanced manner if statistical power, financial considerations, or additional monitoring objectives warrant adjusting the sample size. This scaling ability is an important advantage, as (1) the number of plots per park cannot be adequately estimated a priori (see Section 3.4.2, Hubbard et al. in review) and (2) future changes in technology, objectives, and budgets may necessitate increasing or decreasing sample sizes.

2.2.3 Sampling frame

The sampling frame for Casa Grande Ruins NM includes all terrestrial areas within park boundaries, except for the following (Figure 2-3):

- Roads, buildings, and the visitor picnic area (including 100-m buffer)

- Selected cultural features (such as the Compounds A and B, Great House).

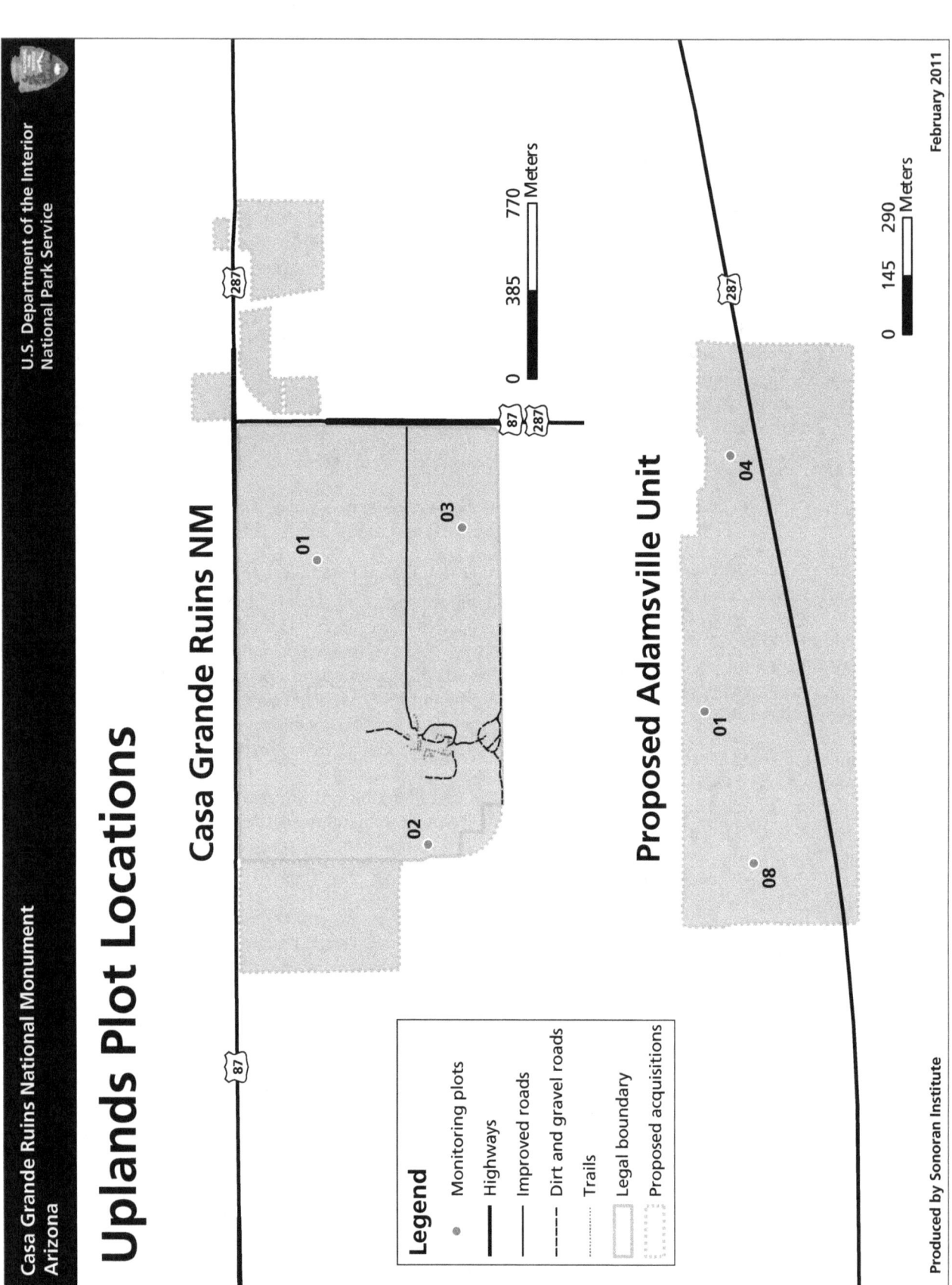

Uplands Plot Locations

Casa Grande Ruins NM

01

03

02

Proposed Adamsville Unit

04

01

08

Legend

- • Monitoring plots
- —— Highways
- —— Improved roads
- ----- Dirt and gravel roads
- ········ Trails
- ☐ Legal boundary
- ☐ Proposed acquisitions

Casa Grande Ruins National Monument
Arizona

U.S. Department of the Interior
National Park Service

0   385   770
Meters

0   145   290
Meters

Produced by Sonoran Institute

February 2011

Figure 2-2. Allocation of monitoring plots, Casa Grande Ruins NM.

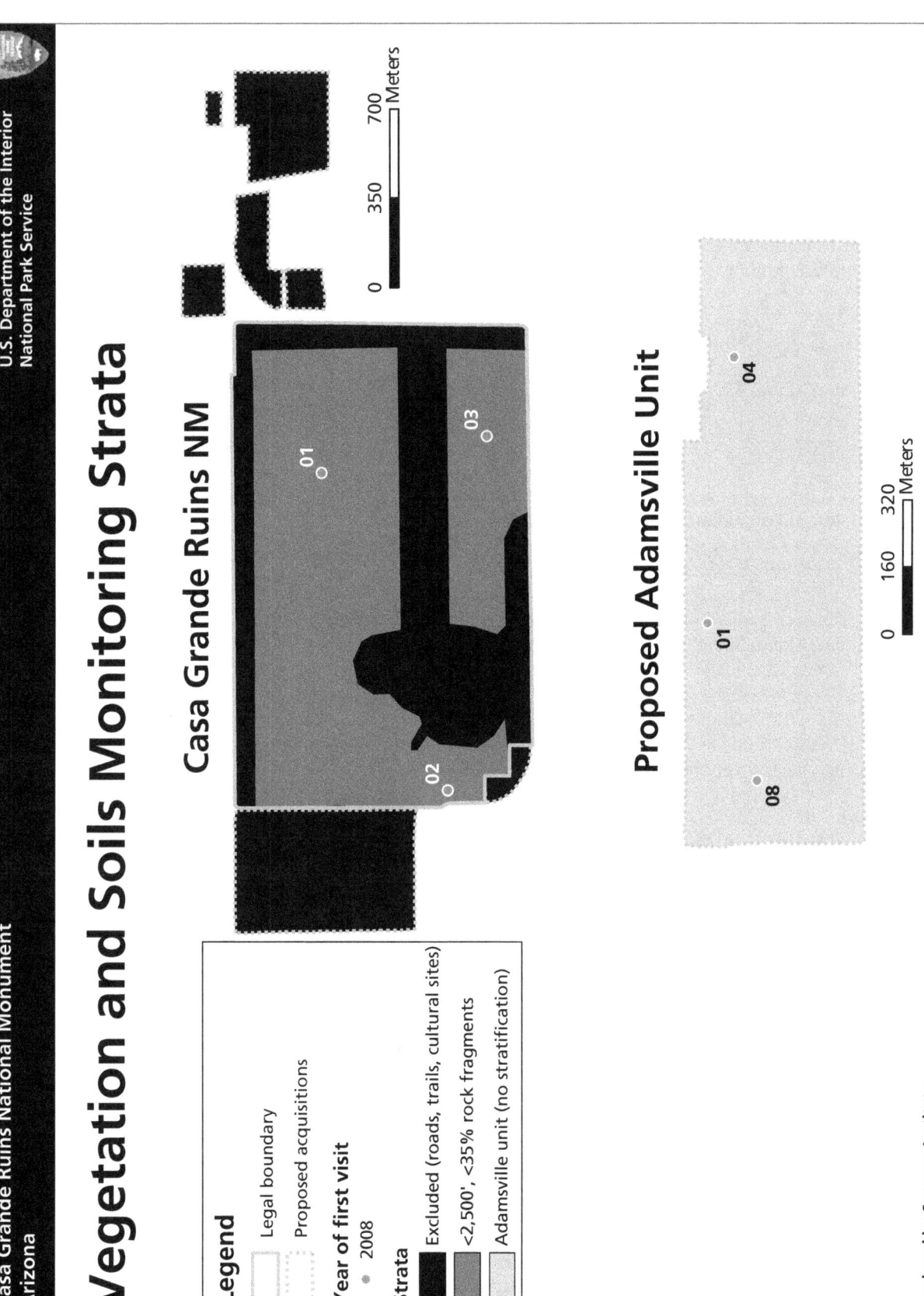

Vegetation and Soils Monitoring Strata

Casa Grande Ruins NM

Proposed Adamsville Unit

Legend

Legal boundary

Proposed acquisitions

Year of first visit

• 2008

Strata

Excluded (roads, trails, cultural sites)

<2,500', <35% rock fragments

Adamsville unit (no stratification)

Produced by Sonoran Institute

February 2011

Figure 2-3. Sampling frame for terrestrial vegetation and soils monitoring, Casa Grande Ruins NM.

The excluded areas listed above comprise 36% of the Casa Grande unit sampling frame. No areas were excluded at the Adamsville unit sampling frame. Other potential expansion areas adjacent to and near the current monument boundary were excluded from the sampling frame. Plot locations at both units were reviewed by Casa Grande Ruins NM archeologists; plots located in sensitive areas were not sampled.

2.2.4 Management assessment points

To achieve the NPS's core mission of resource protection, resource management and monitoring must be explicitly linked (Bingham et al. 2007). We advocate the use of management assessment points as a bridge between science and management. Management assessment points, which are ". . . pre-selected points along a continuum of resource-indicator values where scientists and managers have agreed to stop and assess the status or trend of a resource relative to program goals, natural variation, or potential concerns" (Bennetts et al. 2007), aid interpretation of ecological information within a management context. They do not define strict management or ecological thresholds, inevitably result in management actions, or reflect any legal or regulatory standard; they are only intended to serve as a potential early warning system allowing scientists and managers to pause, review the available information in detail, and consider options. Bennetts and others (2007) have provided a detailed explanation of this concept and its application to monitoring and management of protected areas.

Although no management assessment points have been formally established for Casa Grande Ruins NM, we propose some assessment points here, based on the ecological literature and our knowledge of these ecosystems and park management goals. We intend for these assessment points to (1) initiate a discussion of potential indicators and assessment points and (2) provide a useful framework for evaluating terrestrial vegetation and soils data in a broader ecological and managerial context. Proposed assessment points are summarized in Table 3-4 and discussed in Chapter 4.

2.2.5 Statistical power to distinguish status from management assessment points

Estimating our statistical power to distinguish current conditions (i.e., status) from management assessment points (see Section 2.2.4) is important

for both protocol design (especially determining adequate sample sizes) and data interpretation. Adequate sample size (number of plots) is estimated by (Herrick et al. 2005a):

$$n = \frac{(S)^2 (Z_\alpha + Z_\beta)^2}{(MDC)^2}$$

Where:

S = standard deviation of the sample,

Z_α = Z-coefficient for false change (Type I) error (set at 90%),

Z_β = Z-coefficient for missed-change (Type II) error (set at 10%), and

MDC = minimum detectable change from the assessment point (set at 5–20%).

Bonham (1989), Elzinga and others (1998), and Herrick and others (2005a) provide detailed discussions of statistical power to detect differences from a standard.

2.2.6 Statistical power to detect trends

Statistical power is also important for evaluating trends (change over time) in monitoring parameters. Adequate sample size (number of plots) for detecting a trend of a given size across a landscape with permanent plots is estimated from:

$$n = \frac{(S_{diff})^2 (Z_\alpha + Z_\beta)^2}{(MDC)^2}$$

Where:

S_{diff} = Standard deviation of the differences between paired samples,

Z_α = Z-coefficient for false change (Type I) error (set at 90%),

Z_β = Z-coefficient for missed-change (Type II) error (set at 10%), and

MDC = minimum detectable change size between time 1 and time 2 (set at 5–20%)

In this case, we only have one year of data, so we estimate S_{diff} using the following equation:

$$S_{diff} = (S_1)(\sqrt{(2(1 - corr_{diff}))})$$

Where:

S_1 = Sample standard deviation among sampling units at first time period, and

$corr_{diff}$ = estimated correlation coefficient between time 1 and time 2, set at 0.75.

Bonham (1989), Elzinga and others (1998), and Herrick and others (2005a) provide detailed discussions of statistical power to detect trend.

3 Results

3.1 Vegetation

Creosote bush was the only perennial plant species detected on line-intercept transects at the Casa Grande unit, whereas the Adamsville unit also contained triangle burr ragweed, littleleaf ratany (*Krameria erecta*), and yellow paloverde (*Parkinsonia microphylla*; Table 3-1; tables begin on page 30). Frequency subplots only added one species, candy barrel cactus (*Ferocactus wislizeni*), at the Casa Grande and Adamsville units. No exotic plant species were detected on any of the monitoring plots and transects.

All major lifeforms were encountered on the monitoring plots, with the exception of vines and perennial grasses. The greatest cover occurred in the field elevation stratum (Figure 3-1). Only two species, creosote bush and yellow paloverde, occurred in the subcanopy stratum, while only yellow paloverde occurred in the canopy stratum.

3.2 Soils

3.2.1 Soil stability

3.2.1.1 Casa Grande unit

Valid stability samples were collected from two of the three plots. Because samples at plot V002 were collected when the soil was saturated, they are invalid and are not reported in these results. The two sites with valid measurements had a surface soil stability rating of at least 4.5, which is beyond the midpoint between very unstable and very stable. About two thirds of the samples were in category 6 (very stable) at the Casa Grande unit (Table 3-2). Samples collected from beneath vegetation had stability values slightly lower than those collected in open spaces. Soil stability samples collected from bare ground had a stability rating of around 3. In contrast, samples collected from a light cyanobacteria soil crust substrate had a stability rating of nearly 5. Plot-specific information for the Casa Grande unit is given in Appendix B, Table B3a.

3.1.1.2 Adamsville unit

At the Adamsville unit, all sites had a surface soil stability rating of at least 3.5, which is slightly beyond the midpoint between very unstable and very stable, and about 40% of the samples were in category 6 (very stable) (Table 3-2). Samples collected from beneath vegetation had slightly higher stability values than those collected in open spaces. Soil stability samples collected from bare ground had a stability rating of less than 3. In contrast, samples collected from a light cyanobacteria soil crust substrate had a stability rating of greater than 5. Plot-specific information for the Adamsville unit is provided in Appendix B, Table B3b.

3.2.2 Soil cover

At the Casa Grande unit, soil substrate cover was dominated by light cyanobacteria crusts, bare soil, and plant litter. Twenty percent of the soil surface was bare soil without vegetative cover and 38% of the soil surface was light cyanobacteria crusts without vegetative cover (see Table 3-2). Gravel, light cyanobacteria crusts, and bare soil dominated the soil substrate cover at the Adamsville unit. Eight percent of the soil surface was bare soil without vegetative cover and 16% was light cyanobacteria crusts without vegetative cover. Plot-specific information for the Casa Grande and Adamsville units is provided in Appendix B, Tables B3a and B3b, respectively.

3.2.3 Biological soil crust cover and frequency

At the Casa Grande unit, field-crew members identified six lichen species and one unknown lichen in addition to bryophytes and cyanobacteria crusts to morphological groups within the point-quadrats (Table 3-3). Cover was dominated by light cyanobacteria crusts, and total lichen and dark cyanobacteria cover was low. Cover by bryophytes was extremely low. While total lichen cover was low, *Collema* species were ubiquitous. Lichens with crustose, gelatinous, and squamulose morphologies were found on all three plots. Plot-specific information for the Casa Grande unit is provided in Appendix B, Table B4. Differences in the information on biological soil crusts acquired from the line-point intercept and point-quadrat methodologies will be addressed in Section 4.4; plot-specific information is provided in Appendix B, Table B5. The biological soil crust point-quadrat method was not used at the Adamsville unit.

3.3 Management assessment points

Relevant data were contrasted with proposed management assessment points to assist in the

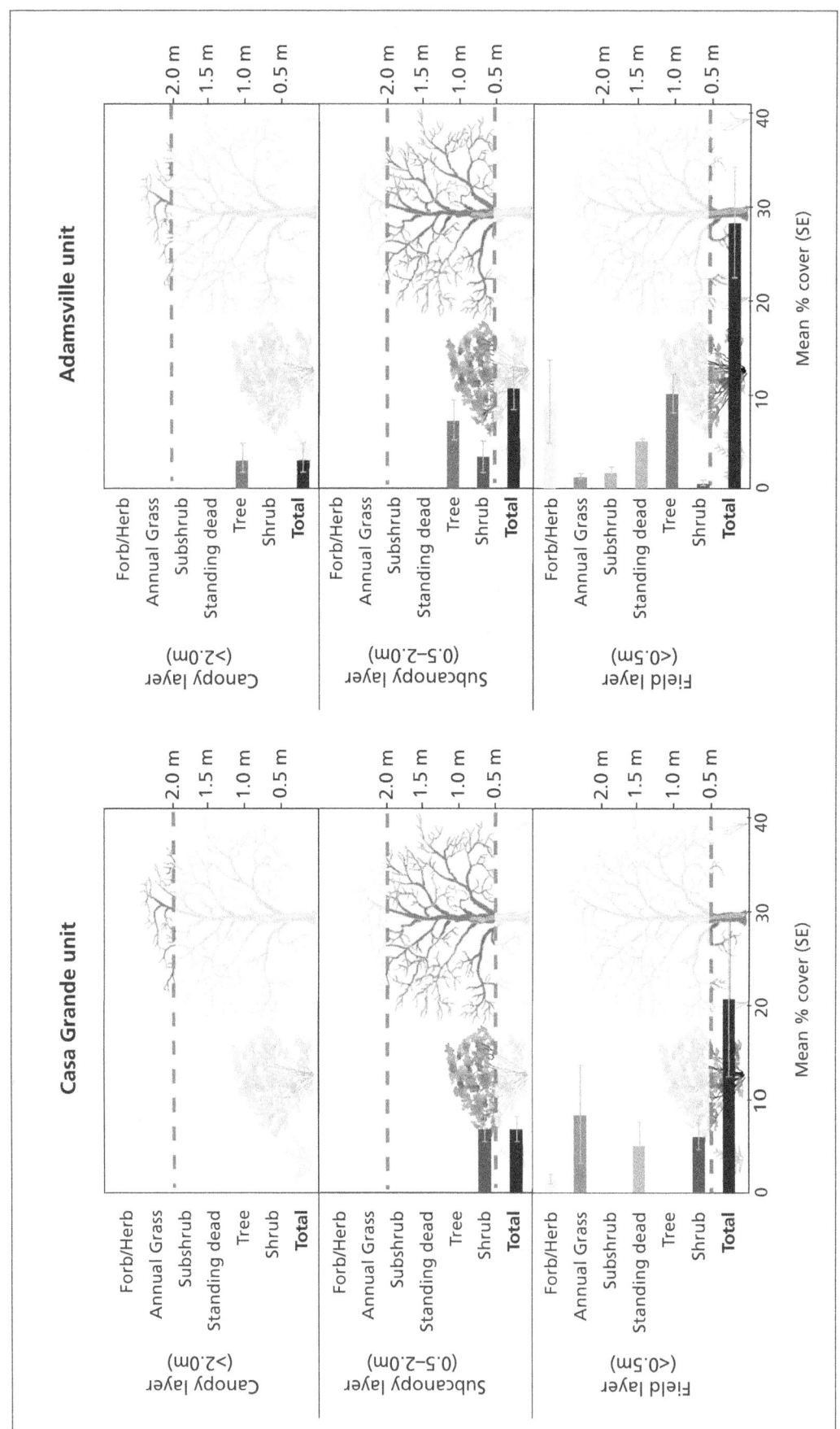

Figure 3-1. Lifeform cover in terrestrial vegetation monitoring plots, Casa Grande Ruins NM, 2008.

interpretation of the monitoring data (Table 3-4). Most indicators did not approach the management assessment points, although some individual plots had values that suggested some potential site-specific issues. For example, plot V001 at the Casa Grande unit exceeded the management assessment point for amount of bare soil without vegetative cover. Plot-specific information is provided in Appendix B, Table B6.

3.4 Estimates of power and species detectability

3.4.1 Power to distinguish monitoring data from management assessment points

Our design permitted us to detect a 5% difference from the management assessment point for site stability parameters, a 10% difference for the bare ground assessment point, and 0.5 index value for the soil aggregate stability assessment point with 90% power and a 10% chance of a false-change error (Table 3-4).

3.4.2 Power to detect trends in plant lifeforms and common perennial species

Our proposed sampling design met our expectations for statistical power to detect trends in lifeforms and common perennial species based on our design criteria (i.e., to detect a 10% change with 90% power and 10% chance of a false-change error). Our data indicate that we will be able to detect a 5% change (absolute foliar cover) for all detected perennial species and one of two plant lifeforms with three or fewer plots each at the Casa Grande and Adamsville units (Ap-

pendix B, Tables B1–B3). However, we will only be assured of detecting a 12% change in annual grasses at the Casa Grande unit, as this lifeform was highly variable in its foliar cover.

3.4.3 Power to detect trends in soil substrate cover

Our proposed sampling design met our expectations for statistical power to detect trends in most substrate cover types based on our design criteria (i.e., to detect a 10% change with 90% power and 10% chance of a false-change error). Our data indicate that we will be able to detect a ≤10% change for 7 of 10 substrate types with three or fewer plots each at the Casa Grande unit and for all 10 substrate types at the Adamsville unit (Appendix B, Table B2). Using three plots at the Casa Grande unit, we will only be assured of detecting an 11%, 23%, and 15% change in bare soil without vegetative cover, light cyanobacteria crusts without vegetative cover, and dark cyanobacteria crusts, respectively, as these substrates were highly variable across the three plots.

Table 3-1. Foliar cover types and minimum detectable change by height category, Casa Grande Ruins NM, 2008.

Species/lifeform	Height category	Mean ± SE	MDC with plots
Casa Grande unit			
Annual Forb	Field (<0.5 m)	1.4% ± 0.61	5% with 1 plot
Annual Grass	*Field (<0.5 m)*	*8.3% ± 5.21*	*12% with 3 plots*
Larrea tridentata (creosote bush)	Field (<0.5 m)	6.0% ± 1.37	5% with 1 plot
	Subcanopy (0.5–2.0 m)	7.5%± 1.46	5% with 2 plots
Snag	Field (<0.5 m)	5.0% ± 2.53	6% with 3 plots
Adamsville unit			
Annual Forb	Field (<0.5 m)	9.2% ± 4.41	10% with 3 plots
Annual Grass	Field (<0.5 m)	1.3% ± 0.24	5% with 1 plot
Ambrosia deltoidea (triangle burr ragweed)	Field (<0.5 m)	1.4% ± 0.73	5% with 1 plot
Krameria erecta (littleleaf ratany)	Field (<0.5 m)	0.3% ± 0.28	5% with 1 plot
Larrea tridentata (creosote bush)	Field (<0.5 m)	10.0% ± 2.08	5% with 3 plots
	Subcanopy (0.5–2.0 m)	7.2% ± 2.16	5% with 3 plots
Parkinsonia microphylla (yellow paloverde)	Field (<0.5 m)	0.6% ± 0.28	5% with 1 plot
	Subcanopy (0.5–2.0 m)	3.3% ± 1.68	5% with 2 plots
	Canopy (>2.0 m)	3.1% ± 1.55	5% with 2 plots
Snag	Field (<0.5 m)	5.0% ± 0.24	5% with 1 plot
Unknown shrub	Field (<0.5 m)	0.6% ± 0.56	5% with 1 plot

"MDC" = minumum detectable change (%). See text for statistical power criteria. Bolded, italicized species and lifeforms failed to meet our 10% change criteria.

Table 3-2. Substrate cover and soil surface aggregate stability by class and minimum detectable change, Casa Grande Ruins NM, 2008.

Parameter	Casa Grande unit		Adamsville unit		Parkwide	
	Mean ± SE	MDC, # plots	Mean ± SE	MDC, # plots	Mean ± SE	MDC, # plots
Substrate						
Bare soil (<2 mm), no overhead cover	20.3% ± 4.9	*11%, 3*	8.1% ± 1.4	5%, 1	14.2% ± 3.5	8%, 6
Bare soil (<2 mm), under vegetation	8.5% ± 3.9	8%, 3	8.1% ± 0.8	5%, 1	8.3% ± 1.8	5%, 4
Light cyanobacteria soil crust, no overhead cover	38.3% ± 10.9	*23%, 3*	15.7% ± 4.7	10%, 3	27.0% ± 7.3	*16%, 6*
Light cyanobacteria soil crust, under vegetation	5.8% ± 2.7	6%, 3	8.5% ± 3.7	8%, 3	7.2% ± 2.1	5%, 5
Annual plant base	0.0% ± 0.0	n/a	3.1% ± 1.9	5%, 2	1.5% ± 1.1	5%, 2
Litter (intact organic matter)	10.4% ± 3.4	8%, 3	4.7% ± 1.2	5%, 1	7.6% ± 2.1	5%, 5
Dark cyanobacteria soil crust	14.0% ± 6.8	*15%, 3*	4.3% ± 1.5	5%, 2	9.2% ± 3.8	8%, 6
Gravel (2–75 mm)	5.0% ± 2.3	5%, 3	43.8% ± 4.8	10%, 3	24.4% ± 9.0	*19%, 6*
Lichen-dominated soil crust	2.9% ± 2.9	7%, 3	2.5% ± 0.8	5%, 1	2.7% ± 1.4	5%, 2
Moss-dominated soil crust	0.3% ± 0.3	5%, 1	0.7% ± 0.5	5%, 1	0.5% ± 0.3	5%, 1
Perennial plant base	0.1% ± 0.1	5%, 1	0.8% ± 0.2	5%, 1	0.5% ± 0.2	5%, 1
Rock (76–600 mm)	0.1% ± 0.1	5%, 1	1.7% ± 1.0	5%, 1	0.9% ± 0.6	5%, 1

Decreasing erosion hazard →

Table 3-2. Substrate cover and soil surface aggregate stability by class and minimum detectable change, Casa Grande Ruins NM, 2008, cont.

Parameter	Casa Grande unit		Adamsville unit		Parkwide	
	Mean ± SE	MDC, # plots	Mean ± SE	MDC, # plots	Mean ± SE	MDC, # plots
Surface Soil Aggregate Stability						
Overall						
Average soil stability*	5.03 ± 0.17	0.9, 3	4.19 ± 0.16	0.4, 3	4.53 ± 0.12	0.6, 5
% samples "very stable" (=6)	64%	15%, 3	43%	10%, 3	51%	13%, 6
Under vegetation						
Average soil stability*	4.66 ± 0.31	1.1, 3	4.38 ± 0.24	0.4, 3	4.46 ± 0.20	0.5, 6
% samples "very stable" (=6)	52%	10%, 3	49%	8%, 3	50%	7%, 6
No vegetation cover						
Average soil stability*	5.20 ± 0.20	0.8, 3	4.01 ± 0.22	0.35, 3	4.57 ± 0.15	0.6, 6
% samples "very stable" (=6)	70%	15%, 3	37%	10%, 3	52%	15%, 6
Substrate = bare soil						
Average soil stability*	3.14 ± 0.80	n/a	2.76 ± 0.33	1, 3	2.83 ± 0.30	0.6, 6
% samples "very stable" (=6)	15%	n/a	29%	18%, 3	18%	12%, 6
Substrate = light cyanobacteria soil crust						
Average soil stability*	4.78 ± 0.24	0.6, 3	4.89 ± 0.18	0.9, 3	4.84 ± 0.15	0.4, 6
% samples "very stable" (=6)	45%	23%, 3	44%	16%, 3	45%	8%, 6
Substrate = gravel						
Average soil stability*	3.44 ± .071	n/a	3.15 ± 0.33	1.5, 3	3.21 ± 0.29	1, 6
% samples "very stable" (=6)	22%	n/a	18%	16%, 3	19%	10%, 6
Substrate = litter						
Average soil stability*	6.0 ± n/a	n/a	4.40 ± 1.03	1.3, 3	4.67 ± 0.88	1, 6
% samples "very stable" (=6)	100%	n/a	60%	15%, 3	67%	22%, 6

* Range 1–6 (very unstable to very stable)

Values are % cover unless otherwise indicated. "MDC" = minumum detectable change (%). See text for statistical power criteria. Bolded, italicized substrates failed to meet our 10% change criteria.

Soil aggregate stability averages for Casa Grande Unit are based on two plots becuase samples for plot V002 are not reported because soil was saturated at time of sampling

Table 3-3. Biological soil crust cover types and frequency by species and morphological group, Casa Grande Ruins NM, 2008.

Species/Morphological group	Lichen growth form	Cover		Within-plot frequency	Landscape frequency
		Mean ± SE	MDC with plots	Mean ± SE	# sites (% of 3)
Amandinea punctata	Crustose lichen	0.83% ± 0.47	5% with 1 plot	39% ± 5	3 (100%)
Candelariella citrina	Crustose lichen	0.12% ± 0.12	5% with 1 plot	6% ± 2	1 (33%)
Collema coccophorum	Gelatinous lichen	2.24% ± 0.62	5% with 1 plot	93% ± 2	3 (100%)
Collema tenax	Gelatinous lichen	0.83% ± 0.50	5% with 1 plot	69% ± 3	3 (100%)
Peltula richardsii	Squamulose lichen	0.58% ± 0.58	5% with 1 plot	7% ± 2	2 (66%)
Placidium lacinulatum	Squamulose lichen	1.25% ± 1.25	5% with 1 plot	57% ± 7	3 (100%)
Unknown lichen	Lichen	0.25% ± 0.25	5% with 1 plot	n/a	n/a
Lichen-dominated soil crust (totals)		*6.09% ± 1.11*	*5% with 1 plot*	*93% ± 2*	*3 (100%)*
Light cyanobacteria soil crust		37.75% ± 10.37	22% with 3 plots	91% ± 2	3 (100%)
Dark cyanobacteria soil crust		2.06% ± 0.90	5% with 1 plot	41% ± 1	3 (100%)
Moss-dominated soil crust		0.25% ± 0.25	5% with 1 plot	9% ± 3	2 (66%)

Point-quadrats were not collected at the Adamsville unit. "MDC" = minimum detectable change (% cover), "n" = required number of plots for power criteria (see text). Values are cover (%) unless otherwise indicated.

Table 3-4. Terrestrial vegetation and soils monitoring data in the context of proposed management assessment points, Casa Grande Ruins NM, 2008.

Issue	Management assessment point (source)	Parkwide measurement				Point met?	Recommendation
		Mean	SE	MDC	n=		
Erosion hazard	Bare ground is >20% (authors' professional judgment)	14.20%	3.50%	8%	6	no	Continue monitoring
	Average surface soil aggregate stability is <3 (authors' professional judgment, based on description in Herrick et al. 2005a)	4.53	0.12	0.60	6	no	Continue monitoring
Site stability	Foliar cover of creosote (*Larrea tridentata*) in field layer is <5% (authors' professional judgment, based on description in Morrison et al. 2003)	7.99%	3.51%	5%	3	no	Continue monitoring
	Foliar cover of creosote in subcanopy layer is <5% (authors' professional judgment, based on description in Morrison et al. 2003)	7.36%	2.86%	5%	2	no	Continue monitoring
Exotic plant dispersal	Extent of exotic plants is >20% (authors' professional judgment, based on overview in NPS 2005)	0%	n/a	n/a	n/a	no	Continue monitoring
Exotic plant invasion	Foliar cover ratio of exotic:native plants is >1:5 (authors' professional judgment, based on overview in NPS 2005)	0%	n/a	n/a	n/a	no	Continue monitoring

"MDC" = minimum detectable change (%), "n" = number of plots to meet power assumptions under our criteria (see text).

4 Discussion

4.1 From mesquite to creosote bush

The "bit of typical desert land" that inspired Frank Pinkley's musings in 1924 has changed much since then. Once described as dominated by mesquite, the dominant vegetation type at the monument today is the creosote bush shrubland alliance, which contains a monoculture of creosote bush and covers approximately 80% of the Casa Grande unit and 30% of the Adamsville unit (Buckley et al. 2009). Overall, the dominance of creosote bush and minimal cover of other perennial species found in this study was consistent with the vegetation characterization results (see Table 1-1). All three of the vegetation and soils monitoring plots at the Casa Grande unit and one plot at the Adamsville unit (V004) fell within the creosote bush shrubland alliance. The remaining two plots at the Adamsville unit were within 40 m of the creosote bush shrubland alliance boundary.

Adamsville plot V001 was in the foothill/yellow paloverde/creosote bush wooded shrubland alliance, 40 m from the boundary of the creosote bush shrubland alliance. Yellow paloverde was present in all three canopy strata and accounted for roughly 10% and 4% cover in the subcanopy and canopy layers, respectively. Adamsville plot V008 was in the creosote bush - [triangle burr ragweed - littleleaf ratany] shrubland alliance and was the only plot to have both triangle burr ragweed and littleleaf ratany. Yellow paloverde was present in all three canopy strata and accounted for roughly 5% cover in the subcanopy and canopy layers.

During the vegetation characterization, field crews mapped 333 live mesquite individuals within the Casa Grande unit (Buckley et al. 2009). The majority of those individuals were concentrated near the Great House, visitor center, maintenance area, and roads. Some of the individuals near park buildings were irrigated horticultural specimens. The mesquites were also clustered in other areas where surface water collects (Buckley et al. 2009). Most of the mesquite locations were excluded from the sampling frame because they were within 100 m of roads, buildings, or selected cultural features. Therefore, it is unsurprising that we did not encounter any mesquite on our monitoring plots despite its presence in the park.

4.2 Biological soil crusts

A community of cyanobacteria, algae, lichens, and bryophytes, known as biological soil crusts, cover much of the soil surface at Casa Grande Ruins NM. The biological soil crust community is dominated by cyanobacteria, typical of the Sonoran Desert. In contrast to the two perennial plant species found on Casa Grande unit plots, field crews identified six species of soil lichens. However, as in many arid regions, the potential abundance and cover of biological soil crusts at Casa Grande Ruins NM is unknown. Percent sand content ranged from 71 to 76% and 59 to 65% at the Casa Grande and Adamsville units, respectively. Therefore, biological soil crusts likely have a minimal impact on infiltration at the Casa Grande unit and a slightly positive impact on infiltration at the Adamsville unit.

Of the six soil lichens identified by field crews at the Casa Grande unit, three fix nitrogen: *Peltula richardsii*, *Collema coccophorum* (Figure 4-1), and *Collema tenax*. The *Collema* species were found on all three plots and averaged nearly 3% cover in the point-quadrats. *Peltula richardsii* occurred on two plots and averaged less than 1% cover in the point-quadrats.

The six lichens found by field crews fall into three lichen growth forms: crustose, gelatinous, and squamulose (Table 4-1).

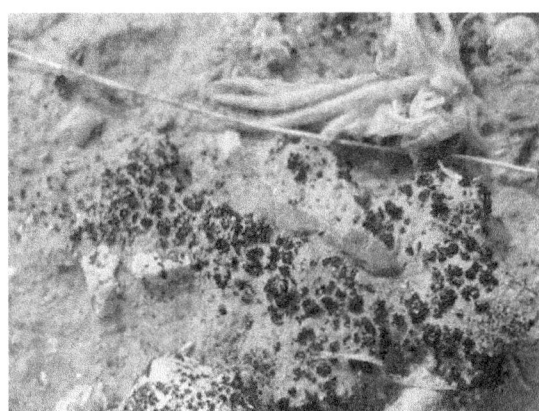

Figure 4-1. *Collema coccophorum* in terrestrial vegetation monitoring plots, Casa Grande Ruins NM, 2008.

Table 4-1. Genera, growth forms, and ecological function of lichens found at Casa Grande Ruins NM, 2008.

Growth form Genera	Description	Ecological function			
		Water erosion protection	Wind erosion protection	Nitrogen fixation	Recovery from disturbance
Crustose *Amandinea, Candelariella*	Lichens forming a crust-like growth that is tightly attached to the substrate.	++	+	some	moderate
Foliose	Three-dimensional lichens. Foliose lichens tend to be flattened, lichens with a definite upper and lower surface.	++	++	some	slow
Fruticose	Three-dimensional lichens. Fruticose lichens tend to be ropey or shrub-like and are sometimes branched.	++	++	some	slow
Gelatinous *Collema*	Lichens with an unlayered thallus becoming jelly-like when wetted. They tend to be blackish in color and turn blue-green when wet. Have an algal partner which is a cyanobacterium which allows them to fix atmospheric nitrogen.	+	+	yes	fast
Squamulose *Peltula, Placidium*	Lichens with thalli occurring as discrete scales, warts or flakes that can be ear-shaped, convex or concave.	+++	++	some	moderate

Eldridge and Rosentreter 1999
The + to +++ range is a general relative scale that describes how well a particular growth form protects the soil from water or wind erosion. +++ provides the most protection.

4.3 Exotic invasive plants

Our data indicate that the current impacts of exotic invasive plants on the terrestrial ecosystems at Casa Grande Ruins NM are negligible. However, recent studies documented 31 invasive plants at the park (see Section 1.5.3). In addition, changing biotic and abiotic conditions may favor the expansion of these species in the future. We will continue to monitor the distribution and abundance of these and other non-native plants, and recommend continued vigilance and the development of a containment strategy that could be employed in the event of a future increase in these potentially problematic species.

4.4 Site and soil stability

Our data indicate that soils at Casa Grande Ruins NM are moderately well-armored, with 14.2 ± 3.5% (see Table 3-2) of the soil surface consisting of exposed bare mineral soil. However, the amount of exposed bare mineral soil tends to be higher at the Casa Grande unit (all sites >15%; at Casa Grande unit plot V001, that number was 30%). In addition, light cyanobacteria soil crusts without vegetation cover composed 38% and 16% of the soil cover at the Casa Grande and Adamsville units, respectively (27% parkwide).

Although the stability of surface soil aggregates was satisfactory relative to our proposed management assessment point (see Table 3-4), the stability of surface aggregates collected from bare soil was below 3, indicating the potential for soil erosion from bare patches. Surface aggregates collected from areas with light cyanobacteria biological soil crusts averaged a stability rating near 5 (stable). Therefore, light cyanobacteria crusts appear to increase surface stability.

Our data on the dynamic factors of water erosion indicated that potential erosion is a moderate concern, which coincides with actual erosion estimates. All plots at the Adamsville unit showed minor signs of rill development over 1–5% of the plot, and plot CAGA_V001 had a gully that affected 1–5% of the plot. In addition, all six plots sampled had signs of burrowing that affected 1–5% of the plot. While current soil loss appears to be moderate and localized, we emphasize the potential impacts that erosion might have on critical cultural resources at Casa Grande Ruins NM.

4.5 Monitoring implications

Because this effort entailed some of the first terrestrial vegetation and soils monitoring in the Sonoran Desert Network, much of our focus was on evaluating the efficacy of the sampling and response designs to support improvement of the protocol. We found the plot sampling design to be efficient. Most plots were sampled within 2–4 hours, including tasks that will not need to be repeated in successive visits (i.e., initial plot layout, permanent marking and mapping, and collection of in situ soil and landscape parameters).

4.5.1 Sample stratification

All plots at the Casa Grande unit are within the 101 strata (<2,500' in elevation, with all surface soils containing <35% rock fragments). Soil was not used to stratify at the Adamsville unit due to the unit's size. However, all plots at the Adamsville unit are on the Gunsight-Pinamt complex soil map unit, which has rock-fragment content of 35–60%. Therefore, the Adamsville-unit plots would have fallen within the 102 strata (<2,500' in elevation, with all surface soils containing 35–60% rock fragments). The lack of stratification at the Adamsville unit, based on soils information, did not impact our design. As a result, we see no compelling reason to reallocate our plots and will continue to separate the Casa Grande-unit (101 strata) plots from the Adamsville-unit plots (102 strata).

Stratifying sampling sites by the two unit classes (Casa Grande and Adamsville) proved an efficient approach for sampling canopy (>2-m stature), subcanopy (0.5–2.0 m), and field-layer (<0.5 m) vegetation at Casa Grande Ruins NM. The approach effectively partitioned variation, providing excellent statistical power for status and trend detection that generally exceeded our design criteria, with one exception: for annual grasses in the field layer at the Casa Grande unit, we can only detect a 12% change in cover with our three plots. The design also effectively captured and differentiated the two distinct vegetation types at the park, as described in Section 4.1.

4.5.2 Overall effectiveness

4.5.2.1 Vegetation

Overall, we were pleased that our design and sample size (6 plots) met or exceeded the statistical power thresholds for vegetation that we had set in our monitoring objectives. Despite relatively high between-plot variation, we also met or exceeded most of our thresholds for substrate type and surface aggregate stability.

We detected only five of 127 species documented in the flora of the park (Powell et al. 2006). While detecting only five perennial species might seem a poor result, we believe it is reasonable, considering that we grouped all annual grasses and forbs, and did not sample areas near roads or selected cultural sites (eliminating 36% of the park from the sampling frame). In addition, the plots fell within sparsely vegetated areas, as described in the recent vegetation characterization effort (Buckley et al. 2006).

4.5.2.2 Substrate

Unfortunately, the design was less effective for sampling substrate cover at the Casa Grande unit. This is likely due to high within-unit variability in substrate cover of bare soil, light cyanobacteria, and dark cyanobacteria substrates, and the difficulty of distinguishing between the substrates (especially when wet, as it was during the Casa Grande unit sampling effort). Increasing our power and precision for bare-soil and dark-cyanobacteria substrates would require three additional plots (a doubling of cost and effort). Increasing our power and precision for light cyanobacteria would require 13 additional plots—a significant increase in cost and effort that seems unwarranted.

In order to help evaluate the protocol, we compared the methods of estimating biological soil crust and substrate cover (line-point intercept and point-quadrat) using paired t-tests in which each plot at the Casa Grande unit was a sample. The two sampling methods resulted in similar values for most of the substrate cover classes (Figure 4-2), but for two of the nine classes, the line-point intercept method yielded significantly higher cover for light cyanobacteria soil crusts and significantly lower cover values for litter (Table 4-2). The differences in cover values likely stem from differences in the methodologies and the patchiness of substrate cover. The point-quadrats were placed along the line-point intercept transects such that no point-quadrat measurements actually occurred along the line-point transect. Given the patchiness of substrate and biological soil crust cover, a difference between measurement locations of 10 cm could result in a different substrate determination. We will continue to compare the methods at other SODN parks

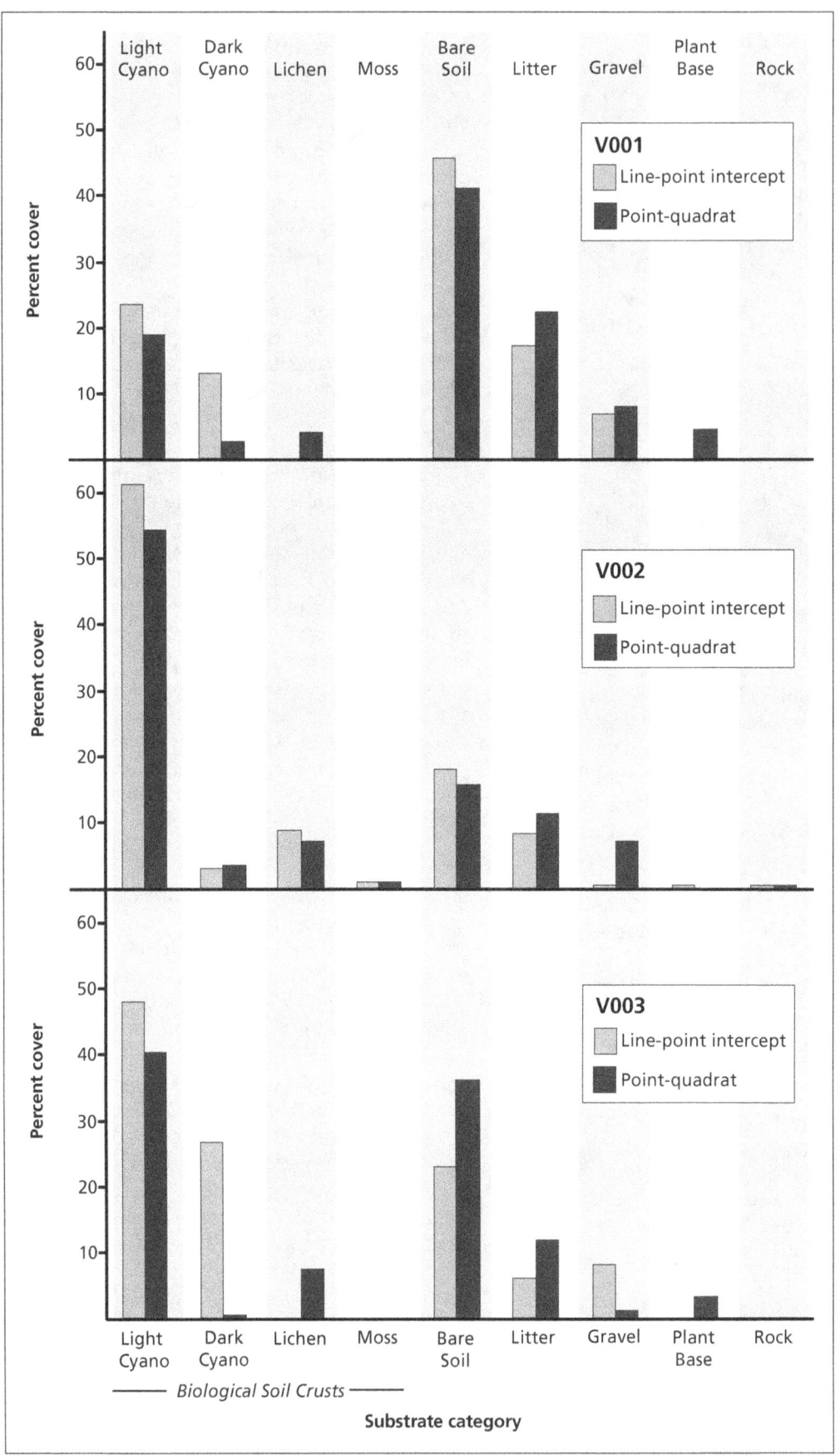

Figure 4-2. Biological soil crust and substrate cover by plot, Casa Grande Ruins NM, 2008.

before making a final determination between the methods to evaluate biological soil crust cover.

4.5.3 Lichen characterization

We are also considering revising the protocol so that lichen biological soil crusts are identified to the lichen growth-form level rather than to species. As described in Section 4.2, lichens can be described by their growth forms, and ecological functions tend to be similar within a given growth form. Identifying lichens by growth form would require less training of field crews and likely would result in increases in repeatability and statistical power and decreases in time and money. However, because some lichens are difficult to place in a growth form group, changes in species composition might go undetected (Eldridge and Rosentreter 1999). Collecting initial data at the species level, as was done in this case, is advantageous because it provides additional information and a broader characterization of the biological soil crust community.

After comparing these results with our monitoring objectives, we conclude that the sampling design is appropriate, and will maintain the same basic approach for future monitoring, with the next sampling in 2013. However, we likely will identify lichens to the growth form level in 2013 and are still evaluating the efficacy of the point-quadrats for biological soil crust and substrate cover.

4.6 Are terrestrial vegetation and soils within the range of natural variability?

Within the context of the network's vital signs for species composition, community structure, and dynamic soil function, we conclude that terrestrial vegetation and soils at Casa Grande Ruins NM are within the range of natural variability given the groundwater depletion that has occurred in the area since the early 1900s. While current park conditions contrast with those described in local and regional historic accounts (recognizing the limitations of historical data), the valley-wide groundwater declines that began in the early 1900s likely changed the potential vegetation at Casa Grande Ruins NM, making some degree of change inevitable.

Table 4-2. Paired t-test results for line-point intercept and point-quadrat methods for biological soil crust and substrate cover measurements, Casa Grande Ruins NM, 2008.

Substrate	Mean difference ± SE	t	P
Biological soil crusts			
Light cyanobacteria soil crust	**6.4% ± 0.9**	**7.16**	**0.019**
Dark cyanobacteria soil crust	12.0% ± 7.7	1.55	0.261
Lichen-dominated soil crust	-3.2% ± 2.6	1.22	0.346
Moss-dominated soil crust	0.03% ± 0.03	1	0.423
Other substrates			
Bare soil (<2 mm)	-2.2% ± 5.6	-0.38	0.737
Litter (intact organic matter)	**-5.7% ± 0.9**	**-5.1**	**0.036**
Gravel (2–75 mm)	-0.3% ± 3.9	-0.08	0.946
Plant base	-2.3% ± 1.4	-1.65	0.241
Rock (76–600 mm)	0.01% ± 0.01	1	0.423

t = Student's t test statistic

P = probability of obtaining a test statistic that is at least as extreme as the observed if the null hypothesis (=no difference) is true

Point-quadrats were not collected at the Adamsville unit. df = 2 for all tests.

Substrates for which results are statistically significant (p<0.05) are bold.

5 Literature Cited

Aber, J., and J. Melillo. 1991. Terrestrial ecosystems. Philadelphia, Pa.: Saunders College Publishing.

Bailey, R. G. 1998. Ecoregions: The ecosystem geography of the oceans and continents. New York: Springer-Verlag Inc.

Bennetts, R. E., J. E. Gross, K. Cahill, C. L. McIntyre, B. B. Bingham, J. A. Hubbard, L. Cameron, and S. L. Carter. 2007. Linking monitoring to management and planning: Assessments points as a generalized approach. The George Wright Forum 24(2):59–77.

Belnap J., and D. Eldridge. 2003. Disturbance and recovery of biological soil crusts. Pages 363–383 in J. Belnap and O. L. Lange, eds., Biological soil crusts: Structure, function, and management. Ecological Studies Series 150, second edition. Berlin, Germany.

Belnap, J., B. Büdel, and O. L. Lange. 2003. Biological soil crusts: Characteristics and distribution. Pages 3–30 in J. Belnap and O. L. Lange, eds., Biological soil crusts: Structure, function, and management. Ecological Studies Series 150, second edition. Berlin, Germany.

Belnap, J., J. H. Kaltenecker, R. Rosentreter, J. Williams, S. Leonard, and D. Eldridge. 2001. Biological soil crusts: Ecology and management. BLM Technical Reference 1730-2. Bureau of Land Management, Denver, Colorado.

Belnap, J., S. L. Phillips, J. E. Herrick, and J. R. Johansen. 2007. Wind erodibility of soils at Fort Irwin, California (Mojave Desert), USA, before and after trampling disturbance: Implications for land management. Earth Surface Processes and Landforms 32:75–84.

Bingham, B. B., R. E. Bennetts, and J. A. Hubbard. 2007. Integrating science and management: the road to Rico-Chico. The George Wright Forum 24(2):21–25.

Bonham, C. D. 1989. Measurements for terrestrial vegetation. New York: Wiley-Interscience.

Brown, J. and S. Archer. 1999. Shrub invasion of grassland: Recruitment is continuous and not regulated by herbaceous biomass or density. Ecology 80(7):2385–2396.

Buckley, S., J. A. Hubbard, S. Studd, S. Drake, M. Villarreal, and J. Greene. 2009. Vegetation classification, distribution, and mapping report: Casa Grande Ruins National Monument. Natural Resource Report NPS/SODN/NRR—2009/158. National Park Service, Fort Collins, Colorado.

Clemensen, A. B. 1992. A centennial history of the first prehistoric reserve: 1892–1992. U.S. Department of the Interior, National Park Service, Washington, D.C.

Davenport, D. W., D. D. Breshears, B. P. Wilcox, and C. D. Allen. 1998. Viewpoint: Sustainability of pinion-juniper ecosystems: A unifying perspective of soil erosion thresholds. Journal of Range Management 51:231–240.

D'Antonio, C. and P. Vitousek. 1992. Biological invasions by exotic grasses, the grass/fire cycle, and global change. Annual Review of Ecology and Systematics: 23:63–87.

Dimmitt, M. A. 2000. Biomes and communities of the Sonoran Desert region. Pages 3–18 in S. J. Phillips and P. W. Comus, eds., A natural history of the Sonoran Desert. Tucson: Arizona-Sonora Desert Museum Press.

Eldridge, D. J. and R. Rosentreter. 1999. Morphological groups: A framework for monitoring microphytic crusts in arid landscape. Journal of Arid Environments 41:11–25.

Elzinga, C. L., D. W. Salzer, and J. W. Willoughby. 1998. Measuring and monitoring plant populations. BLM Technical Reference 1730-1. Bureau of Land Management, Denver, Colorado.

Gray, S. T. 2008. Framework for linking climate, resource inventories and ecosystem monitoring. Natural Resource Technical Report NPS/GRYN/NRTR—2008/110. National Park Service, Fort Collins, Colorado.

Halvorson, W. L., and P. Guertin. 2003. USGS Weeds in the west; Status of introduced plants in southern Arizona parks. http://sdfsnet.srnr.arizona.edu/index.php?page=datamenu&lib=2&sublib=13. Last accessed February 10, 2011.

Hendricks, D. M. 1985. Arizona soils. College of Agriculture. University of Arizona, Tucson.

Herrick, J. E., J. W. Van Zee, K. M. Havstad, L. M. Burkett, and W. G. Whitford. 2005a. Monitoring manual for grassland, shrubland and savanna ecosystems. Volume I: Quick start. USDA-ARS Jornada Experimental Range, Las Cruces, New Mexico.

——.2005b. Monitoring manual for grassland, shrubland, and savanna ecosystems. Volume II: Design, supplementary methods, and interpretation. Tucson: University of Arizona Press.

Hubbard, J. A., C. L. McIntyre, S. E. Studd, T. W. Nauman, D. Angell, M. K. Connor, and K. Beaupré. in review. Terrestrial vegetation and soils monitoring protocol and standard operating procedures for the Sonoran Desert Network.

Hubbard, J. A., K. Legg, D. Hubbard, and C. Moss. 2007. Integrated resource management: applying the concepts of Rico and Chico to connect cultural and natural resource management. The George Wright Forum 24(2):94–107.

Ingram, M. 2000. Desert storms. Pages 41–50 in S. J. Phillips and P. W. Comus, eds., A natural history of the Sonoran Desert. Tucson: Arizona-Sonora Desert Museum Press.

McAuliffe, J. R. 1999. The Sonoran Desert: Landscape complexity and ecological diversity. Pages 68–114 in R. H. Robichaux, ed., Ecology of Sonoran Desert plants and plant communities. Tucson: University of Arizona Press.

Morrison, P. H., H. M. Smith IV, and S. D. Snetsinger. 2003. The natural communities and ecological condition of the Sonoran Desert National Monument and adjacent areas. Pacific Biodiversity Institute, Winthrop, Washington.

National Climatic Data Center (NCDC). 2011. Daily surface data for Casa Grande National Monument weather station. http://www4.ncdc.noaa.gov/cgi-win/wwcgi.dll?WWDI~getstate~USA. Last accessed February 10, 2011.

National Park Service (NPS). 2005. Sonoran Desert Network monitoring plan. National Park Service, Sonoran Desert Network, Tucson, Arizona.

——.2009. Strategic plan for natural resource inventories: FY 2008– FY 2012. Natural Resource Report NPS/NRPC/NRR—2009/094. National Park Service, Fort Collins, Colorado.

——.2010a. NPScape landcover measure–Phase 1 metrics processing SOP: Landcover area per category, natural vs. converted landcover, landcover change, and impervious surface metrics. National Park Service, Natural Resource Program Center. Fort Collins, Colorado. Natural Resource Report. NPS/NRPC/IMD/NRR—2010/252. Published Report-2165449.

——.2010b. NPScape housing measure–Phase 1 metrics processing SOP: Current housing density, historic housing density, and projected housing density metrics. National Park Service, Natural Resource Program Center. Fort Collins, Colorado. Natural Resource Report. NPS/NRPC/IMD/NRR—2010/251. Published Report-2165448.

——.2011a. Integrated pest management plan, environmental assessment, Casa Grande Ruins National Monument. http://parkplanning.nps.gov/document.cfm?parkID=36&projectID=24951&documentID=38400. Last accessed February 10, 2011.

——.2011b. Casa Grande Ruins National Monument annual park visitation. http://www.nature.nps.gov/stats/park.cfm?parkid=173. Last accessed February 10, 2011.

Nauman, T. In review. Soil inventory results and relationships to vegetation monitoring data at Casa Grande Ruins National Monument, Arizona.

Powell, B. F., E.W. Albrecht, C. A. Schmidt, W. L. Halvorson, P. Anning and K. Docherty. 2006. Vascular plant and vertebrate inventory of Casa Grande Ruins National Monument. USGS OFR 2005-1185. USGS Southwest Biological Science Center, Sonoran Desert Research Station, University of Arizona, Tucson.

Reichhardt, K. 1992. Natural vegetation of Casa Grande Ruins National Monument, Arizona. Cooperative National Park Resources Studies Unit. Technical Report NPS/WRUA/NRTR—92/45.

Sheppard, P. R., A. C. Comrie, G. D. Packin, K. Angersbach, and M. K. Hughes. 2002. The climate of the U.S. Southwest. Climate Research 21:219–238.

Shinneman, D. J., and W. L. Baker. 2009. Environmental and climatic variables as potential drivers of post-fire cover of cheatgrass (*Bromus tectorum*) in seeded and unseeded semi-arid ecosystems. International Journal of Wildland Fire 18:191–202.

Stehman, S. V. 1999. Basic probabilistic sampling for thematic mapper accuracy assessment. International Journal of Remote Sensing 20:2347–2366.

Studd, S. E., and C. L. McIntyre. 2007. Invasive plant mapping inventory at Casa Grande Ruins National Monument, Arizona. Natural Resource Technical Report Natural Resource Report NPS/IMR/SODN—2007/001. National Park Service, Denver, Colorado.

Swann, D. E., W. W. Shaw, and C. R. Schwalbe. 1994. Assessment of animal damages to archaeological resources at Casa Grande Ruins National Monument. Final report to Southern Arizona Group, U.S. Department of the Interior, National Park Service, Phoenix, Arizona.

Theobald, D. M., D. L. Stevens, Jr., D. White, N. S. Urquart, A. R. Olsen, and J. B. Norman. 2007. Using GIS to generate spatially balanced designs for natural resource applications. Environmental Management 40:134–146.

U.S. Census Bureau, Population Division (USCB). 2011. Table 4. Annual Estimates of the resident population for incorporated places in Arizona: April 1, 2000 to July 1, 2009 (SUB-EST2009-04-04). http://www.census.gov/popest/cities/cities.html. Last accessed February 12, 2011.

Warren, S. D. 2003. Synopsis: Influence of biological soil crusts on arid land hydrology and soil stability. Pages 349–360 in J. Belnap and O. L. Lange, eds., Biological soil crusts: Structure, function, and management. Ecological Studies Series 150, second edition. Berlin, Germany.

Whittaker, R. H. 1975. Communities and ecosystems. Indianapolis, In.: MacMillan.

Wilson, W. 1918. Casa Grande Ruins National Monument enabling legislation. Presidential Proc. No. 1470, Aug. 3, 40 Stat. 1818.

Appendix A. Maps and Photos of Permanent Plots

Casa Grande Ruins National Monument
Arizona

U.S. Department of the Interior
National Park Service

Permanent plot photos: CAGR_V101_001

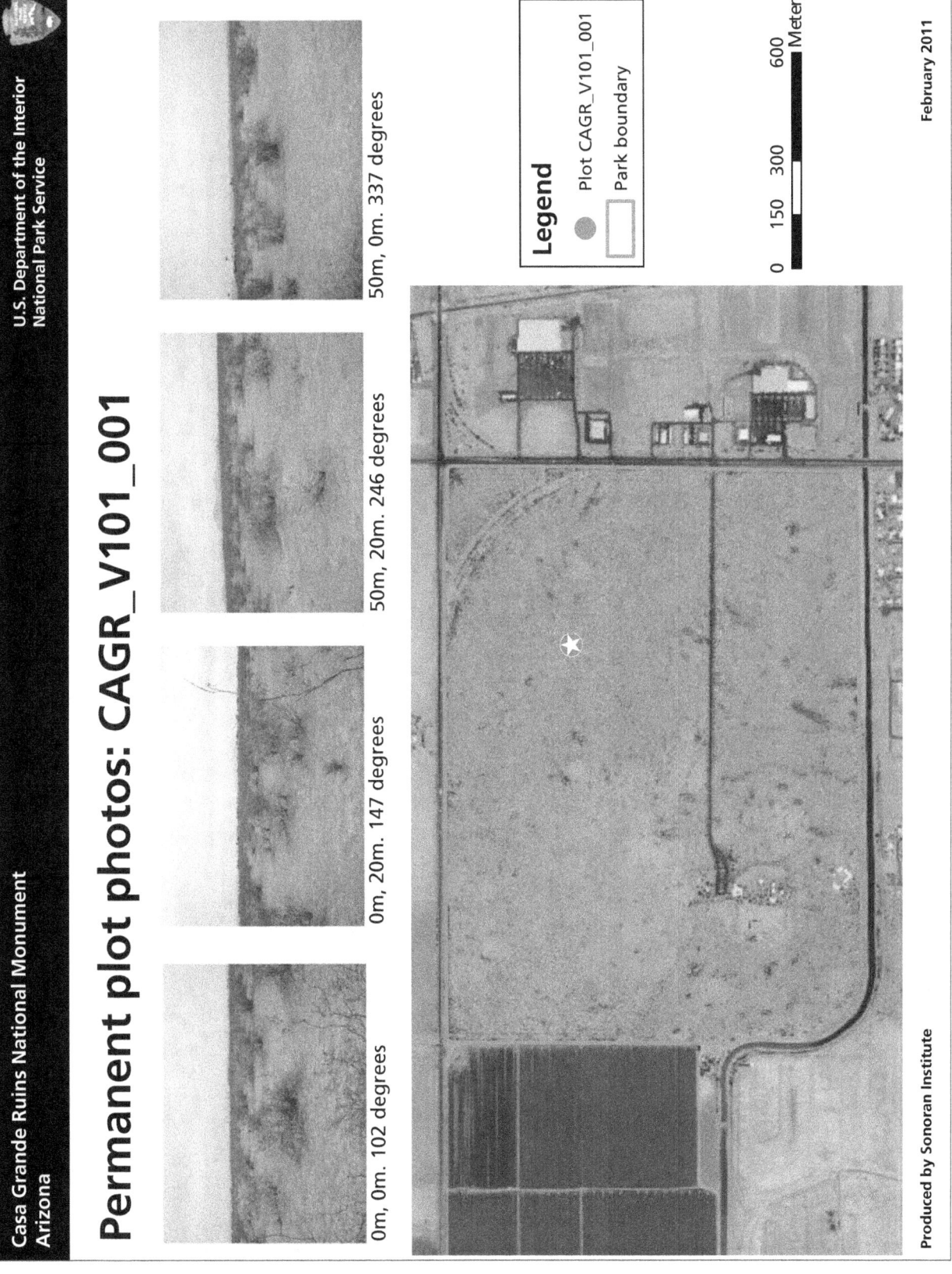

0m, 0m. 102 degrees

0m, 20m. 147 degrees

50m, 20m. 246 degrees

50m, 0m. 337 degrees

Legend

Plot CAGR_V101_001

Park boundary

0   150   300   600
                    Meters

Produced by Sonoran Institute

February 2011

Permanent plot photos: CAGR_V101_002

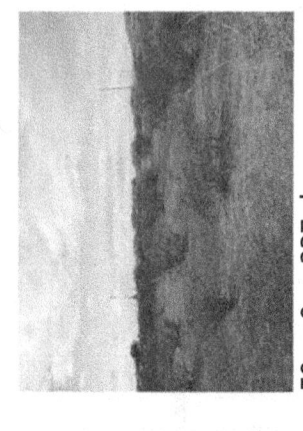

0m, 0m. 346 degrees

0m, 20m. 53 degrees

50m, 20m. 129 degrees

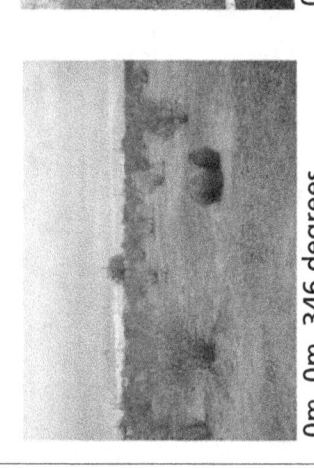

50m, 0m. 237 degrees

Legend

 Plot CAGR_V101_002

Park boundary

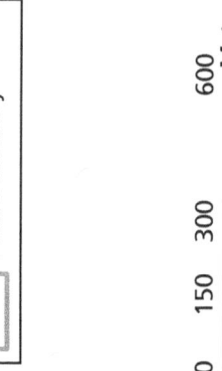

Meters

0   150   300   600

February 2011

Produced by Sonoran Institute

Permanent plot photos: CAGR_V101_003

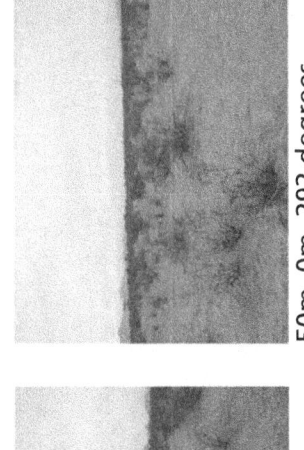

0m, 0m. 50 degrees

0m, 20m. 116 degrees

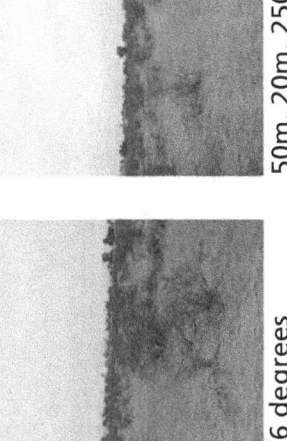

50m, 20m. 250 degrees

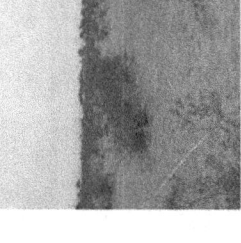

50m, 0m. 292 degrees

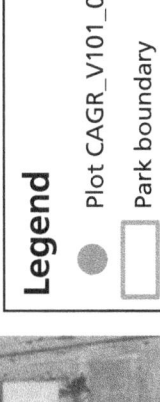

Legend

● Plot CAGR_V101_003

☐ Park boundary

0   150   300   600

Meters

February 2011

Produced by Sonoran Institute

Permanent plot photos: CAGA_V100_001

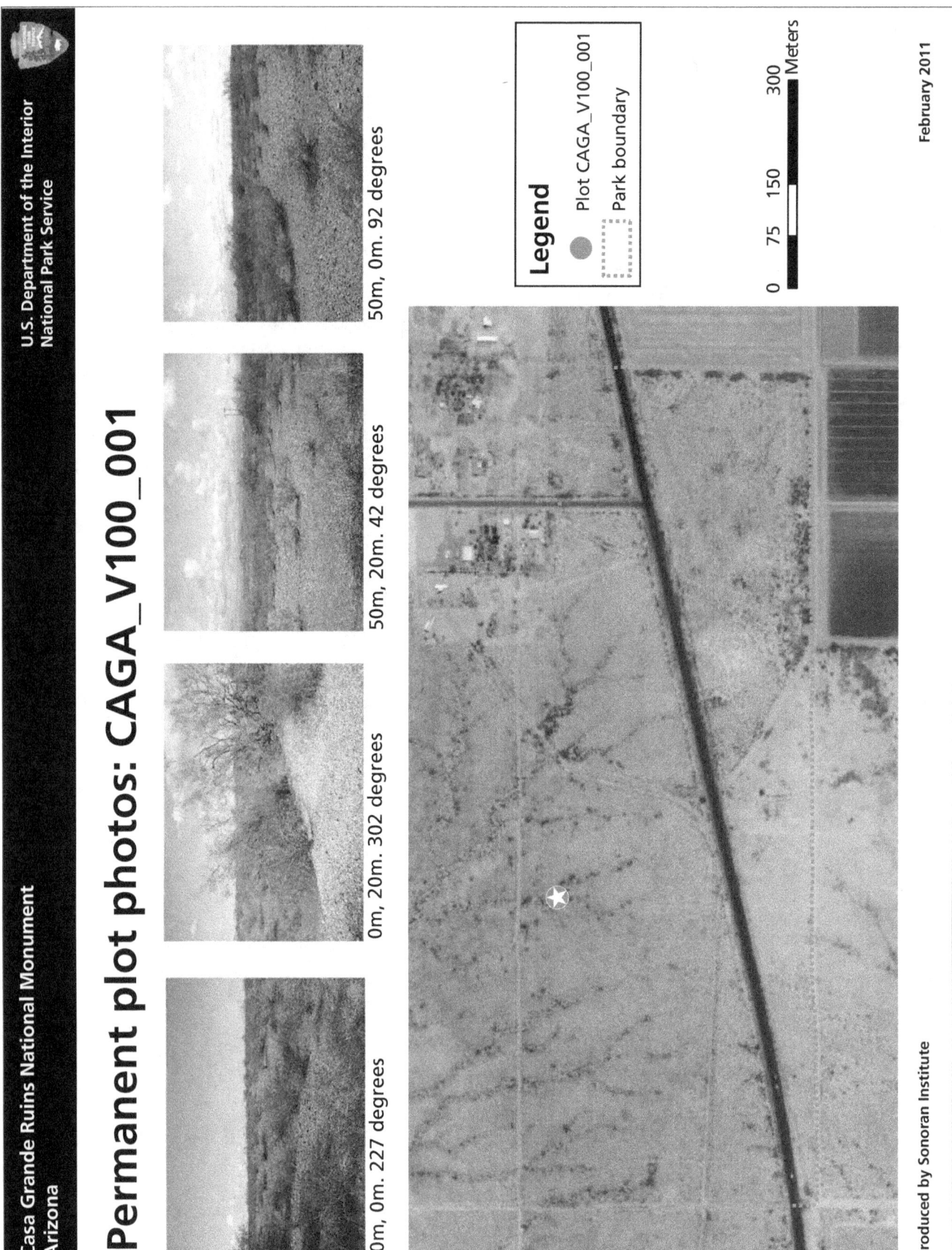

0m, 0m. 227 degrees

0m, 20m. 302 degrees

50m, 20m. 42 degrees

50m, 0m. 92 degrees

Legend

● Plot CAGA_V100_001

⬚ Park boundary

0   75   150   300
Meters

February 2011

Produced by Sonoran Institute

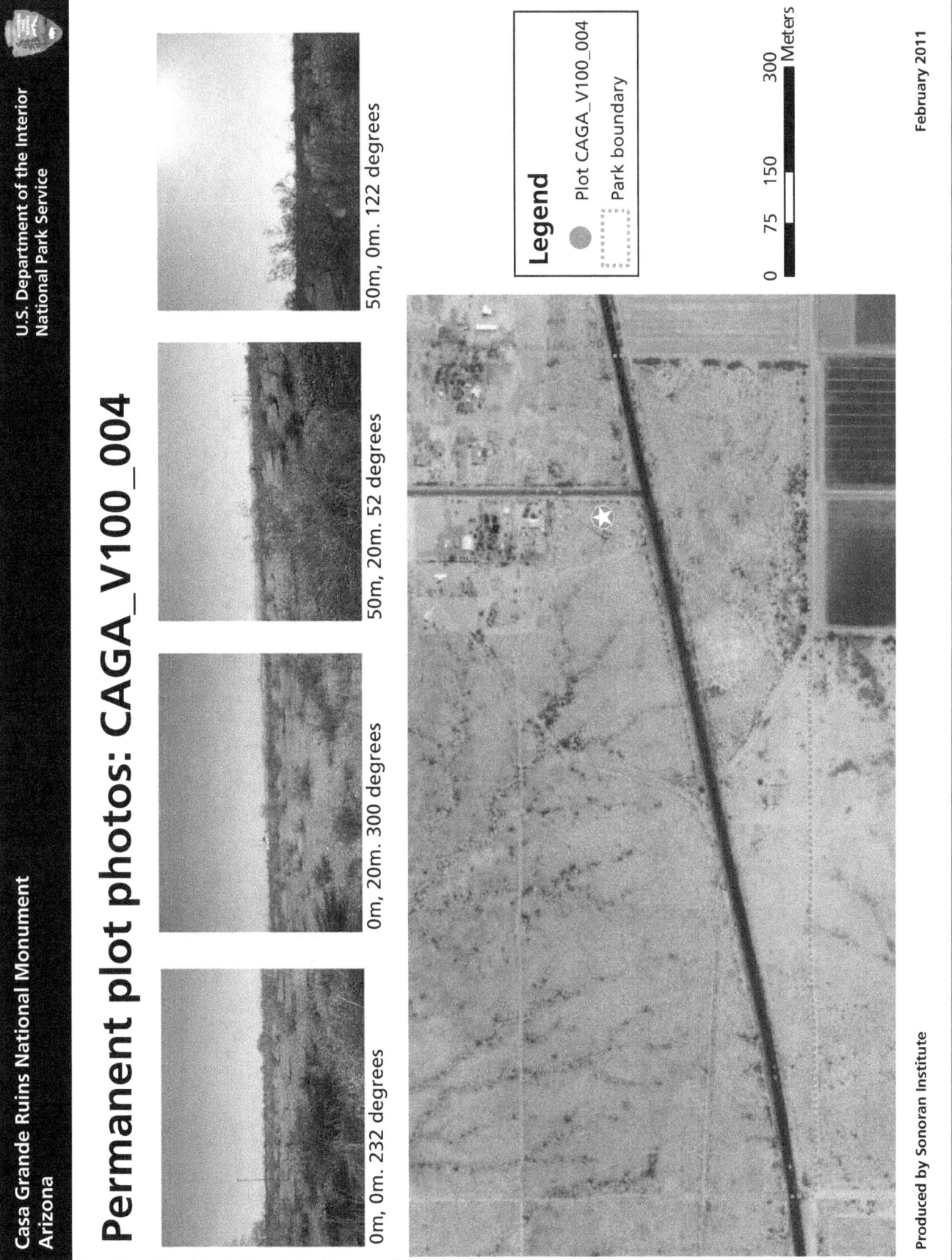

Casa Grande Ruins National Monument
Arizona

U.S. Department of the Interior
National Park Service

Permanent plot photos: CAGA_V100_004

0m, 0m. 232 degrees

0m, 20m. 300 degrees

50m, 20m. 52 degrees

50m, 0m. 122 degrees

Legend

⬤ Plot CAGA_V100_004

⬚⬚⬚ Park boundary

0   75   150   300
Meters

Produced by Sonoran Institute

February 2011

Casa Grande Ruins National Monument
Arizona

U.S. Department of the Interior
National Park Service

Permanent plot photos: CAGA_V100_008

0m, 0m. 232 degrees

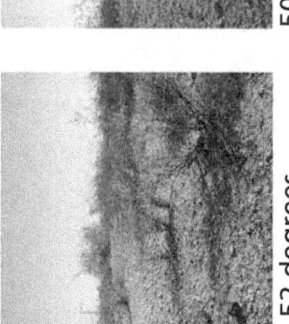

0m, 20m. 300 degrees

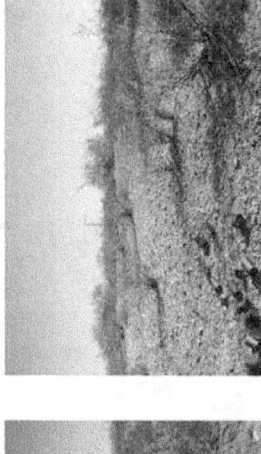

50m, 20m. 52 degrees

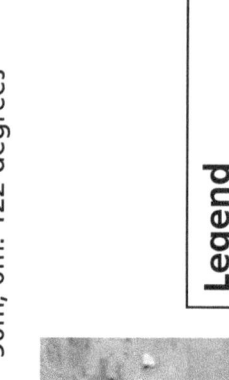

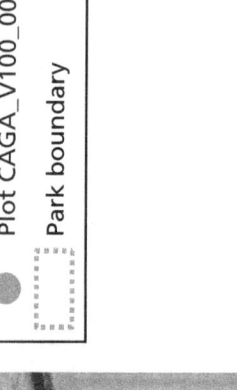

50m, 0m. 122 degrees

Legend

⬤ Plot CAGA_V100_008

⌐ ⌐ Park boundary

0   75   150   300
                            Meters

February 2011

Produced by Sonoran Institute

Appendix B. Supplementary Tables

Table B1. Foliar cover by height category, Casa Grande Ruins NM, 2008.

Code	Species/Lifeform	Common name	Individual unit measures			Across-plot measures					
			V001	V002	V003	AVG	STD	SE	Sdiff	MDC	n=
Casa Grande Unit											
Field layer (<0.5 m)											
AF	Annual Forb		2.08%	0.42%	1.67%	1.39%	0.87%	0.50%	0.61%	0.05	1
AG	Annual Grass		17.92%	0.00%	7.08%	8.33%	9.02%	5.21%	6.38%	0.12	3
LARTRI	*Larrea tridentata*	creosote bush	7.92%	3.33%	6.67%	5.97%	2.37%	1.37%	1.68%	0.05	1
SNAG	Snag		4.58%	0.83%	9.58%	5.00%	4.39%	2.53%	3.10%	0.06	3
Subcanopy layer (<0.5–2.0 m)											
LARTRI	*Larrea tridentata*	creosote bush	9.17%	4.58%	8.75%	7.50%	2.53%	1.46%	1.79%	0.05	2
Adamsville Unit			V001	V004	V008						
Field layer (<0.5 m)											
AF	Annual Forb		7.50%	17.50%	2.50%	9.17%	7.64%	4.41%	5.40%	0.1	3
AG	Annual Grass		1.67%	0.83%	1.25%	1.25%	0.42%	0.24%	0.29%	0.05	1
AMBDEL	*Ambrosia deltoidea*	triangle burr ragweed	0.00%	2.50%	1.67%	1.39%	1.27%	0.73%	0.90%	0.05	1
KRAERE	*Krameria erecta*	littleleaf ratany	0.00%	0.00%	0.83%	0.28%	0.48%	0.28%	0.34%	0.05	1
LARTRI	*Larrea tridentata*	creosote bush	12.08%	12.08%	5.83%	10.00%	3.61%	2.08%	2.55%	0.05	3
PARMIC	*Parkinsonia microphylla*	yellow paloverde	0.83%	0.00%	0.83%	0.56%	0.48%	0.28%	0.34%	0.05	1
SNAG	Snag		5.42%	5.00%	4.58%	5.00%	0.42%	0.24%	0.29%	0.05	1
UNKSHR	Unknown shrub		1.67%	0.00%	0.00%	0.56%	0.96%	0.56%	0.68%	0.05	1
Subcanopy layer (<0.5–2.0 m)											
LARTRI	*Larrea tridentata*	creosote bush	9.58%	9.17%	2.92%	7.22%	3.73%	2.16%	2.64%	0.05	3
PARMIC	*Parkinsonia microphylla*	yellow paloverde	5.42%	0.00%	4.58%	3.33%	2.92%	1.68%	2.06%	0.05	2
Canopy layer (>2.0 m)											
PARMIC	*Parkinsonia microphylla*	yellow paloverde	4.17%	0.00%	5.00%	3.06%	2.68%	1.55%	1.89%	0.05	2

"MDC" = minumum detectable change (%), "n" = number of plots required to meet our power criteria (see text).

Table B2. Within-plot and landscape frequency for all species sampled on monitoring plots, Casa Grande Ruins NM, 2008.

Species	Within-plot frequency (0–5)			(%) Mean	SE	Landscape frequency
Casa Grande Unit	V001	V002	V003			
Shrubs						
Larrea tridentata	5	2	5	80%	20.0%	3 (100%)
Subshrubs						
Ambrosia deltoidea	0	0	0	0%	0.0%	0 (0%)
Krameria erecta	0	0	0	0%	0.0%	0 (0%)
Trees						
Parkinsonia microphylla	0	0	0	0%	0.0%	0 (0%)
Succulents						
Ferocactus wislizeni	0	2	0	13%	13.3%	1 (33%)
Adamsville Unit	V001	V004	V008			
Shrubs						
Larrea tridentata	5	5	5	100%	0.0%	3 (100%)
Subshrubs						
Ambrosia deltoidea	0	5	3	53%	29.1%	2 (67%)
Krameria erecta	0	0	2	13%	13.3%	1 (33%)
Trees						
Parkinsonia microphylla	2	1	2	33%	6.7%	3 (100%)
Succulents						
Ferocactus wislizeni	0	0	1	7%	6.7%	1 (33%)
Parkwide (6 plots)						
Shrubs						
Larrea tridentata				90%	10.0%	6 (100%)
Subshrubs						
Ambrosia deltoidea				27%	17.6%	2 (33%)
Krameria erecta				7%	6.7%	1 (17%)
Trees						
Parkinsonia microphylla				17%	8.0%	3 (50%)
Succulents						
Ferocactus wislizeni				10%	6.8%	2 (33%)

Table B3a. Soil substrate cover and surface aggregate stability class by monitoring plot, Casa Grande Unit.

	Individual plot measures			Across-plot measures				
Parameter	V001	V002	V003	Avg	SD	Sdiff	MDC	# plots
Substrate								
Bare soil (<2 mm), no overhead cover	30.0%	15.8%	15.0%	20.3%	8.4%	5.96%	0.11	3
Bare soil (<2 mm), under vegetation	15.4%	2.1%	7.9%	8.5%	6.7%	4.73%	0.08	3
Light cyanobacteria soil crust, no overhead cover	20.4%	57.9%	36.7%	38.3%	18.8%	13.30%	0.23	3
Light cyanobacteria soil crust, under vegetation	2.9%	3.3%	11.3%	5.8%	4.7%	3.32%	0.06	3
Annual plant base	0.0%	0.0%	0.0%	0.0%	0.0%	0.00%	0.05	0
Litter (intact organic matter)	17.1%	8.3%	5.8%	10.4%	5.9%	4.18%	0.08	3
Dark cyanobacteria soil crust	12.9%	2.9%	26.4%	14.0%	11.8%	8.37%	0.15	3
Gravel (2–75 mm)	6.7%	0.4%	7.9%	5.0%	4.0%	2.84%	0.05	3
Lichen-dominated soil crust	0.0%	8.8%	0.0%	2.9%	5.1%	3.57%	0.07	3
Moss-dominated soil crust	0.0%	0.8%	0.0%	0.3%	0.5%	0.34%	0.05	1
Perennial plant base	0.0%	0.4%	0.0%	0.1%	0.2%	0.17%	0.05	1
Rock (76–600 mm)	0.0%	0.4%	0.0%	0.1%	0.2%	0.17%	0.05	1

Decreasing erosion hazard →

Table B3a. Soil substrate cover and surface aggregate stability class by monitoring plot, Casa Grande Unit, cont.

Parameter	Individual plot measures			Across-plot measures				
	V001	V002	V003	Avg	SD	Sdiff	MDC	# plots
Surface Soil Aggregate Stability								
Overall								
Average soil stability	4.53	-	5.52	5.03	0.699	0.494	0.9	3
SE	0.28	-	0.15	-	-	-	-	-
% samples "very stable" (=6)	55%	-	73%	64%	12%	9%	15%	3
n	47	-	48	-	-	-	-	-
Under vegetation								
Average soil stability	4.12	-	5.42	4.77	0.919	0.650	1.1	3
SE	0.54	-	0.26	-	-	-	-	-
% samples "very stable" (=6)	47%	-	58%	53%	8%	6%	10%	3
n	17	-	12	-	-	-	-	-
No vegetation cover								
Average soil stability	4.77	-	5.56	5.16	0.558	0.394	0.8	3
SE	0.32	-	0.18	-	-	-	-	-
% samples "very stable" (=6)	60%	-	78%	69%	13%	9%	15%	3
n	30	-	36	-	-	-	-	-
Substrate = bare soil								
Average soil stability	3.15	-	n/a	3.15	n/a	n/a	n/a	n/a
SE	0.80	-	n/a	-	-	-	-	-
% samples "very stable" (=6)	29%	-	n/a	29%	n/a	n/a	n/a	3
n	7	-	0	-	-	-	-	-
Substrate = light cyanobacteria soil crust								
Average soil stability	4.38	-	5.04	4.71	0.467	0.330	0.6	3
SE	0.46	-	0.26	-	-	-	-	-
% samples "very stable" (=6)	44%	-	46%	45%	1%	1%	2%	3
n	16	-	24	-	-	-	-	-
Substrate = gravel								
Average soil stability	3.44	-	n/a	3.44	n/a	n/a	n/a	n/a
SE	0.71	-	n/a	-	-	-	-	-
% samples "very stable" (=6)	22%	-	n/a	22%	n/a	n/a	n/a	n/a
n	9	-	0	-	-	-	-	-
Substrate = litter								
Average soil stability	6.00	-	n/a	6.00	n/a	n/a	n/a	n/a
SE	n/a	-	n/a	-	-	-	-	-
% samples "very stable" (=6)	100%	-	n/a	100%	n/a	n/a	n/a	n/a
n	1	-	0	-	-	-	-	-

"n" = number of samples collected per plot.

Table B3b. Soil substrate cover and surface aggregate stability class by monitoring plot, Adamsville Unit.

	Individual plot measures			Across-plot measures				
Parameter	**V001**	**V004**	**V008**	**Avg**	**SD**	**Sdiff**	**MDC**	**# plots**
Substrate								
Bare soil (<2 mm), no overhead cover	6.7%	6.7%	10.8%	8.1%	2.4%	1.70%	0.05	1
Bare soil (<2 mm), under vegetation	7.5%	9.6%	7.1%	8.1%	1.3%	0.95%	0.05	1
Light cyanobacteria soil crust, no overhead cover	6.3%	20.4%	20.4%	15.7%	8.2%	5.78%	0.1	3
Light cyanobacteria soil crust, under vegetation	3.8%	15.8%	5.8%	8.5%	6.5%	4.57%	0.08	3
Annual plant base	6.7%	0.4%	2.1%	3.1%	3.2%	2.29%	0.05	2
Litter (intact organic matter)	5.0%	6.7%	2.5%	4.7%	2.1%	1.48%	0.05	1
Dark cyanobacteria soil crust	5.0%	1.4%	6.4%	4.3%	2.6%	1.82%	0.05	2
Gravel (2–75 mm)	52.9%	36.7%	41.7%	43.8%	8.3%	5.89%	0.1	3
Lichen-dominated soil crust	1.7%	1.7%	4.2%	2.5%	1.4%	1.02%	0.05	1
Moss-dominated soil crust	1.7%	0.4%	0.0%	0.69%	0.9%	0.61%	0.05	1
Perennial plant base	1.3%	0.4%	0.8%	0.83%	0.4%	0.29%	0.05	1
Rock (76–600 mm)	3.8%	0.4%	0.8%	1.7%	1.8%	1.28%	0.05	1

Decreasing erosion hazard →

Table B3b. Soil substrate cover and surface aggregate stability class by monitoring plot, Adamsville Unit, cont.

Parameter	Individual plot measures			Across-plot measures				
	V001	V004	V008	Avg	SD	Sdiff	MDC	# plots
Surface Soil Aggregate Stability								
Overall								
Average soil stability	4.49	4.17	3.92	4.19	0.287	0.203	0.4	3
SE	0.26	0.28	0.30	-	-	-	-	-
% samples "very stable" (=6)	51%	42%	35%	43%	8%	6%	10%	3
n	47	48	48	-	-	-	-	-
Under vegetation								
Average soil stability	4.59	4.50	4.00	4.36	0.32	0.225	0.4	3
SE	0.35	0.41	0.48	-	-	-	-	-
% samples "very stable" (=6)	37%	50%	45%	44%	7%	5%	8%	3
n	27	20	22	-	-	-	-	-
No vegetation cover								
Average soil stability	4.35	3.93	3.85	4.04	0.27	0.191	0.35	3
SE	0.41	0.37	0.37	-	-	-	-	-
% samples "very stable" (=6)	50%	36%	38%	41%	8%	5%	10%	3
n	20	28	26	-	-	-	-	-
Substrate = bare soil								
Average soil stability	3.50	2.50	1.92	2.64	0.799	0.565	1	3
SE	0.46	1.19	0.42	-	-	-	-	-
% samples "very stable" (=6)	25%	25%	0%	17%	14%	10%	18%	3
n	16	4	13	-	-	-	-	-
Substrate = light cyanobacteria soil crust								
Average soil stability	4.71	5.38	4.83	4.97	0.36	0.253	0.5	3
SE	0.35	0.38	0.25	-	-	-	-	-
% samples "very stable" (=6)	43%	63%	39%	48%	13%	9%	16%	3
n	14	8	23	-	-	-	-	-
Substrate = gravel								
Average soil stability	1.00	3.44	2.25	2.23	1.22	0.863	1.5	3
SE	0.00	0.33	1.25	-	-	-	-	-
% samples "very stable" (=6)	0%	19%	25%	15%	13%	9%	16%	3
n	2	27	4	-	-	-	-	-
Substrate = litter								
Average soil stability	5.00	n/a	3.50	4.25	1.06	0.750	1.3	3
SE	1.00	n/a	2.50	-	-	-	-	-
% samples "very stable" (=6)	67%	n/a	50%	59%	12%	9%	15%	3
n	3	0	2	-	-	-	-	-

"n" = number of samples collected per plot.

Table B3c. Soil substrate cover and surface aggregate stability class by monitoring plot, all units.

Decreasing erosion hazard

Parameter	Avg	SD	Sdiff	MDC	# plots
Substrate					
Bare soil (<2 mm), no overhead cover	14.2%	8.7%	6.15%	0.08	6
Bare soil (<2 mm), under vegetation	8.3%	4.3%	3.05%	0.05	4
Light cyanobacteria soil crust, no overhead cover	27.0%	17.9%	12.69%	0.16	6
Light cyanobacteria soil crust, under vegetation	7.2%	5.3%	3.71%	0.05	5
Annual plant base	1.5%	2.6%	1.87%	0.05	2
Litter (intact organic matter)	7.6%	5.0%	3.57%	0.05	5
Dark cyanobacteria soil crust	9.2%	9.3%	6.60%	0.08	6
Gravel (2–75 mm)	24.4%	22.0%	15.57%	0.19	6
Lichen-dominated soil crust	2.7%	3.3%	2.36%	0.05	2
Moss-dominated soil crust	0.5%	0.7%	0.47%	0.05	1
Perennial plant base	0.5%	0.5%	0.34%	0.05	1
Rock (76–600 mm)	0.9%	1.4%	1.01%	0.05	1
Surface Soil Aggregate Stability					
Overall					
Average soil stability	4.53	0.611	0.432	0.6	5
% samples "very stable" (=6)	51%	14%	0.10	13%	6
Under vegetation					
Average soil stability	4.53	0.557	0.394	0.5	6
% samples "very stable" (=6)	48%	8%	0.05	7%	6
No vegetation cover					
Average soil stability	4.49	0.700	0.495	0.6	6
% samples "very stable" (=6)	52%	17%	0.12	15%	6
Substrate = bare soil					
Average soil stability	2.77	0.701	0.495	0.6	6
% samples "very stable" (=6)	20%	13%	0.09	12%	6
Substrate = light cyanobacteria soil crust					
Average soil stability	4.87	0.373	0.264	0.3	7
% samples "very stable" (=6)	47%	9%	0.07	8%	6
Substrate = gravel					
Average soil stability	2.53	1.166	0.824	1	6
% samples "very stable" (=6)	17%	11%	0.08	10%	6
Substrate = litter					
Average soil stability	4.83	1.258	0.890	1	7
% samples "very stable" (=6)	72%	25%	0.18	22%	6

"n" = number of samples collected per plot.

Table B4. Within-plot cover values for biological soil crust species and morphological groups measured in point-quadrats, Casa Grande Ruins NM, 2008.

Species	Morphological group	Simplified morphological group	Individual plot measures			Across-plot measures					
			V001	V002	V003	AVG	STD	SE	Sdiff	MDC	n=
Amandinea punctata	Crustose lichen	Lichen	1.8%	0.4%	0.4%	0.8%	0.8%	0.5%	0.6%	5%	1
Candelariella citrina	Crustose lichen	Lichen	0.3%	0.0%	0.0%	0.1%	0.2%	0.1%	0.1%	5%	1
Subtotal crustose lichen			2.1%	0.4%	0.4%	0.9%	1.0%	0.6%	0.7%	5%	1
Placidium lacinulatum	Squamulose lichen	Lichen	0.0%	3.7%	0.0%	1.2%	2.2%	1.3%	1.5%	5%	1
Peltula richardsii	Squamulose lichen	Lichen	0.0%	0.0%	1.7%	0.6%	1.0%	0.6%	0.7%	5%	1
Subtotal squamulose lichen			0.0%	3.7%	1.7%	1.8%	1.9%	1.1%	1.3%	5%	1
Collema coccophorum	Gelatinous lichen	Lichen	1.8%	1.5%	3.5%	2.2%	1.1%	0.6%	0.8%	5%	1
Collema tenax	Gelatinous lichen	Lichen	0.0%	0.7%	1.7%	0.8%	0.9%	0.5%	0.6%	5%	1
Subtotal gelatinous lichen			1.8%	2.2%	5.2%	3.1%	1.9%	1.1%	1.3%	5%	1
Unknown lichen	Lichen	Lichen	0.0%	0.8%	0.0%	0.2%	0.4%	0.2%	0.3%	5%	1
Moss	Bryophyte	Bryophyte	0.0%	0.7%	0.0%	0.2%	0.4%	0.2%	0.3%	5%	1
	Dark Cyanobacteria	Dark Cyanobacteria	2.5%	3.4%	0.3%	2.1%	1.6%	0.9%	1.1%	5%	1
	Light Cyanobacteria	Bareground / Undifferentiated	18.7%	54.3%	40.3%	37.7%	18.0%	10.4%	12.7%	22%	3
	Bareground	Bareground / Undifferentiated	40.8%	15.7%	36.1%	30.9%	13.3%	7.7%	9.4%	16%	3
		Lichen	3.9%	7.1%	7.3%	6.1%	1.9%	1.1%	1.4%	5%	1
		Bryophyte	0.0%	0.7%	0.0%	0.2%	0.4%	0.2%	0.3%	5%	1
		Dark Cyanobacteria	2.5%	3.4%	0.3%	2.1%	1.6%	0.9%	1.1%	5%	1
		Bareground / Undifferentiated	59.5%	70.0%	76.4%	68.6%	8.5%	4.9%	6.0%	11%	3

"MDC" = minimum detectable change (% cover), "n" = required number of plots for power criteria (see text).

Table B5. Comparison of biological soil crust and substrate measurements between line-point intercept and point-quadrat methodologies, Casa Grande unit, Casa Grande Ruins NM, 2008.

Substrate	Method	Individual plot measures			Across-plot measures		
		V001	V002	V003	Mean	SE	MDC with plots
Biological Soil Crusts							
Light cyanobacteria soil crust	LPI	23.3%	61.3%	47.9%	44.2%	11.1%	23% with 3 plots
	PQ	18.7%	54.3%	40.3%	37.8%	10.4%	22% with 3 plots
Dark cyanobacteria soil crust	LPI	12.9%	2.9%	26.4%	14.0%	6.8%	15% with 3 plots
	PQ	2.5%	3.4%	0.3%	2.1%	0.9%	5% with 1 plot
Lichen-dominated soil crust	LPI	0.0%	8.8%	0.0%	2.9%	2.9%	7% with 3 plots
	PQ	3.9%	7.1%	7.3%	6.1%	1.1%	5% with 1 plot
Moss-dominated soil crust	LPI	0.0%	0.8%	0.0%	0.3%	0.3%	5% with 1 plot
	PQ	0.0%	0.7%	0.0%	0.3%	0.3%	5% with 1 plot
Other Substrates							
Bare soil (<2 mm)	LPI	45.4%	17.9%	22.9%	28.8%	8.5%	18% with 3 plots
	PQ	40.8%	15.7%	36.1%	30.9%	7.7%	16% with 3 plots
Litter (intact organic matter)	LPI	17.1%	8.3%	5.8%	10.4%	3.4%	8% with 3 plots
	PQ	22.2%	11.2%	11.8%	15.1%	3.6%	8% with 3 plots
Gravel (2–75mm)	LPI	6.7%	0.4%	7.9%	3.4%	2.3%	5% with 3 plots
	PQ	7.7%	7.1%	1.0%	5.3%	2.1%	5% with 3 plots
Plant base	LPI	0.0%	0.4%	0.0%	0.1%	0.1%	5% with 3 plots
	PQ	4.2%	0.0%	3.1%	2.2%	1.3%	5% with 3 plots
Rock (76–600mm)	LPI	0.0%	0.4%	0.0%	0.1%	0.1%	5% with 3 plots
	PQ	0.0%	0.4%	0.0%	0.1%	0.1%	5% with 3 plots

LPI = line-point intercept
PQ = point-quadrat
Point-quadrats were not collected at the Adamsville unit.

Table B6. Plot-specific monitoring data in the context of proposed management assessment points, Casa Grande Ruins NM, 2008.

Issue	Management assessment point	Casa Grande unit			Adamsville unit		
		V001	V002	V003	V001	V004	V008
Erosion hazard	Bare ground is >20%	30.0%	15.8%	15.0%	6.7%	6.7%	10.8%
	Average surface soil aggregate stability is <3	4.53	*	5.52	4.49	4.17	3.92
Site stability	Foliar cover of creosote (*Larrea tridentata*) in field layer is <5%	7.92%	3.33%	6.67%	12.08%	12.08%	5.83%
	Foliar cover of creosote in subcanopy layer is <5%	9.17%	8.75%	4.58%	9.58%	9.17%	2.92%
Exotic plant dispersal	Extent of exotic plants is >20%	0.0%	0.0%	0.0%	0.0%	0.0%	0.0%
Exotic plant invasion	Foliar cover ratio of exotic:native plants is >1:5	0.0%	0.0%	0.0%	0.0%	0.0%	0.0%

Plots exceeding a management assessment point appear in bolded red.

*Soil aggregate stability samples for plot V002 are not reported because soil was saturated at time of sampling.

NPS 303/109705, September 2011

National Park Service
U.S. Department of the Interior

Natural Resource Stewardship and Science
1201 Oak Ridge Drive, Suite 150
Fort Collins, Colorado 80525

www.nature.nps.gov

EXPERIENCE YOUR AMERICA™